Real World
Colouring Book
For Advanced Users & Adults

50 Images

Created From Real Life Photos
For You To Colour As You Please.

ISBN 978-0-359-97204-3

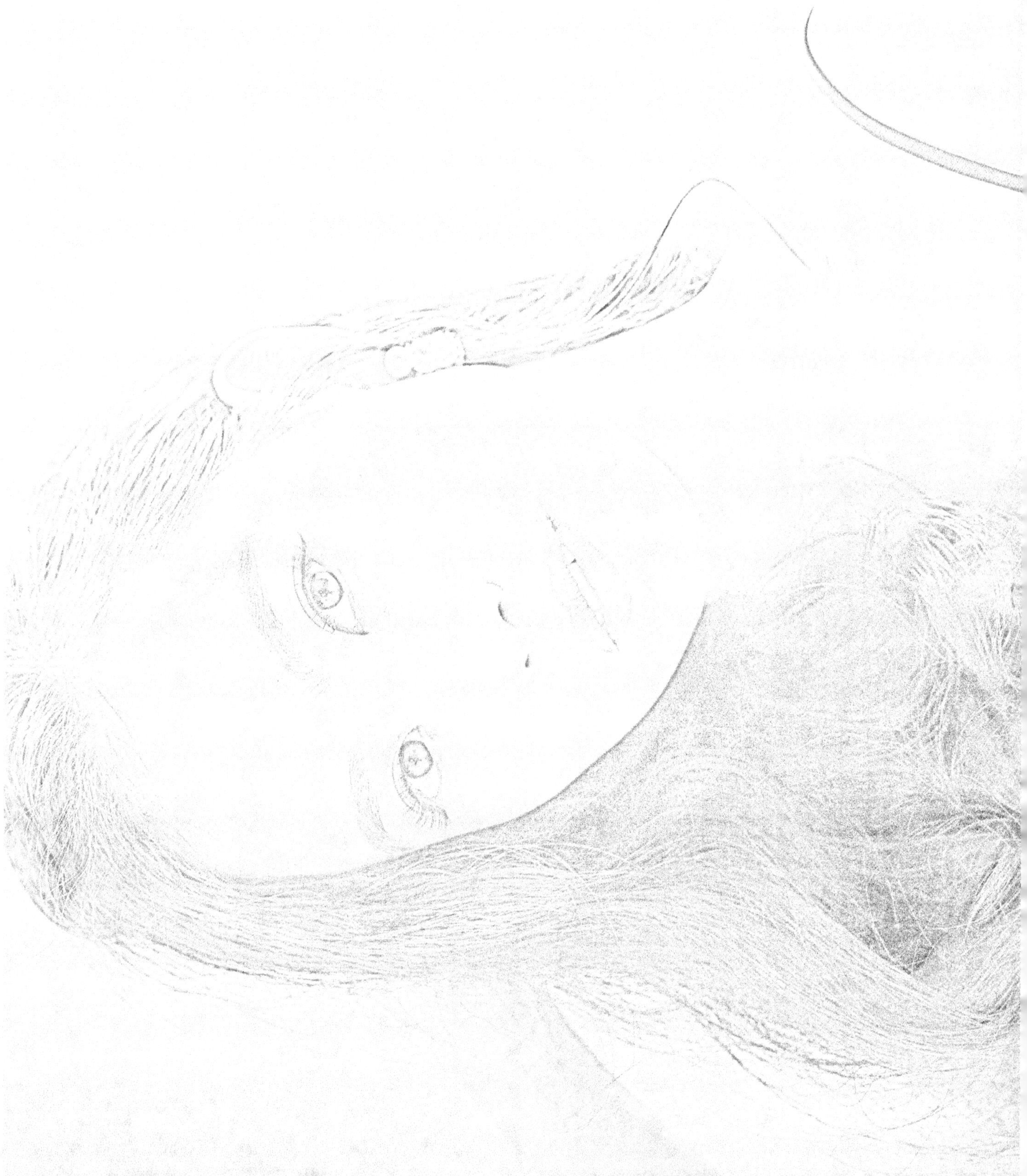

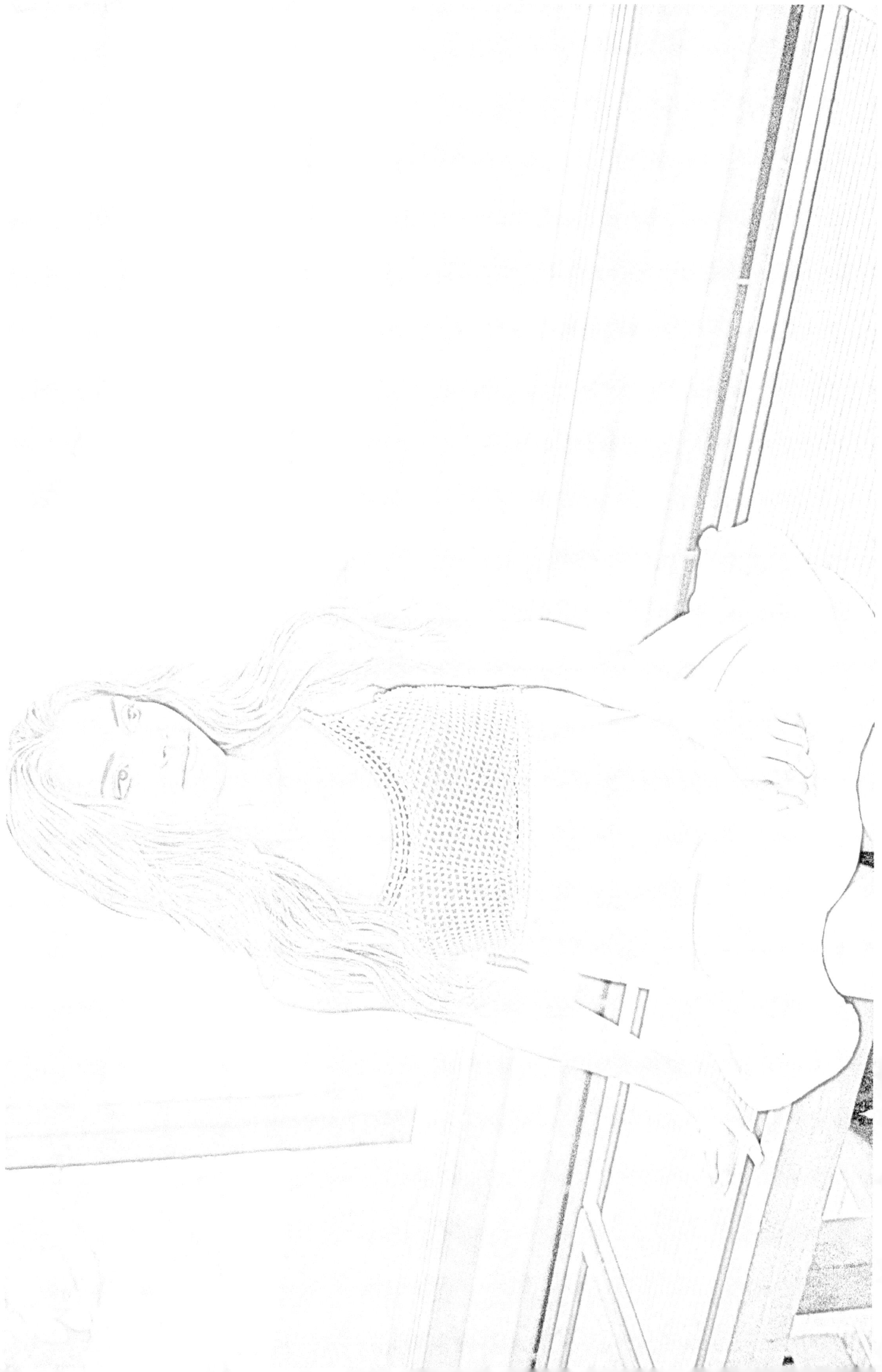

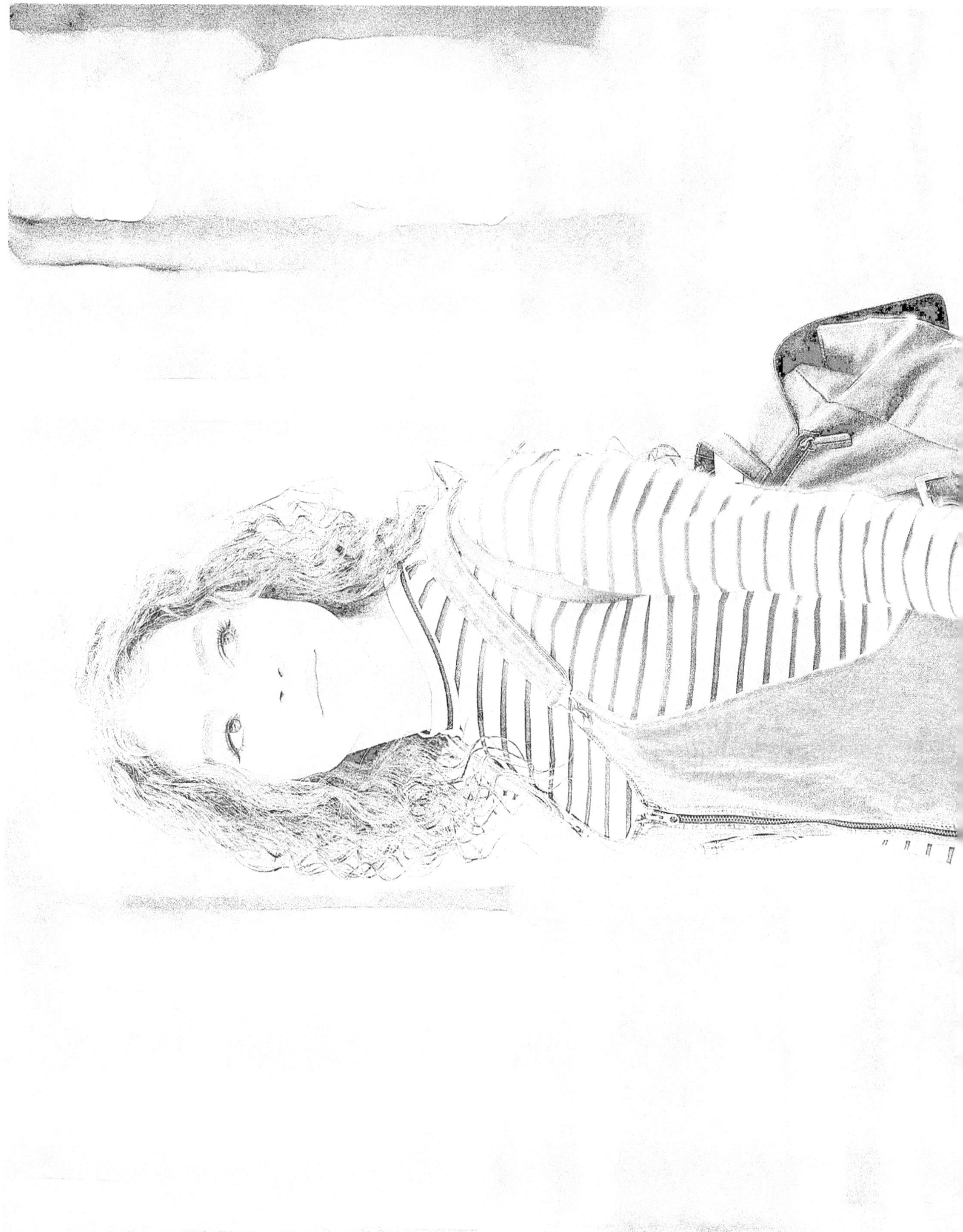

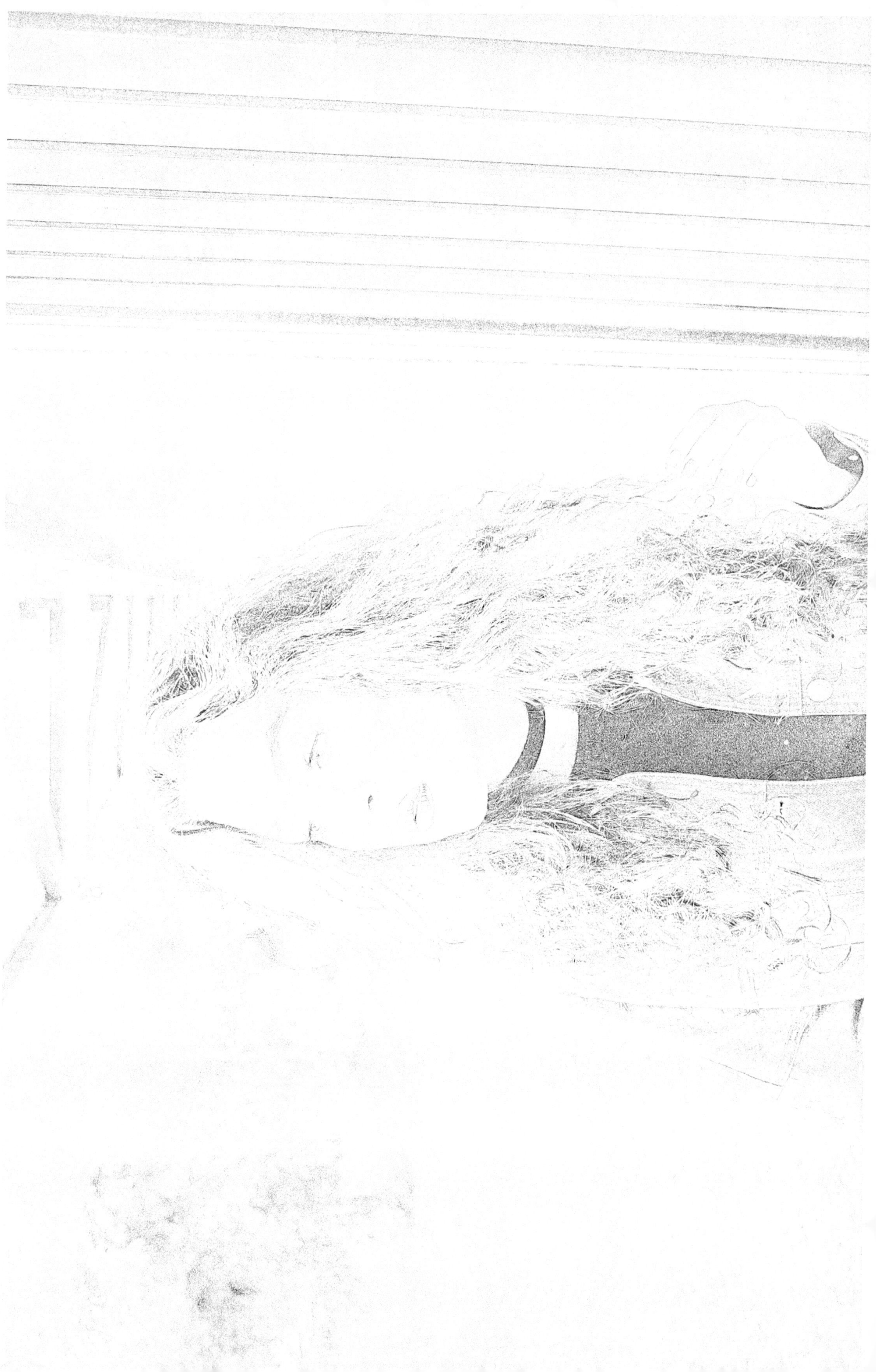

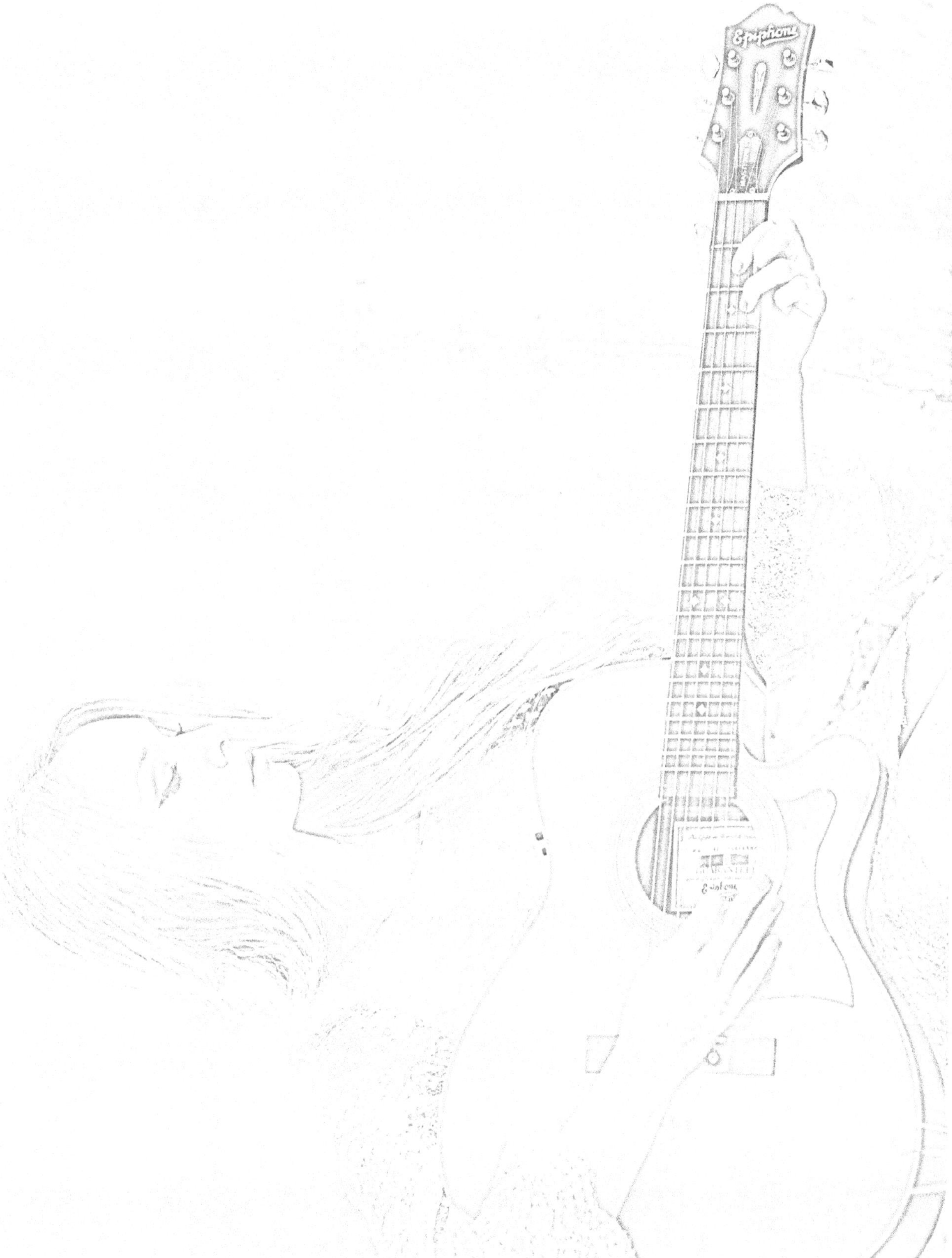
Epiphone

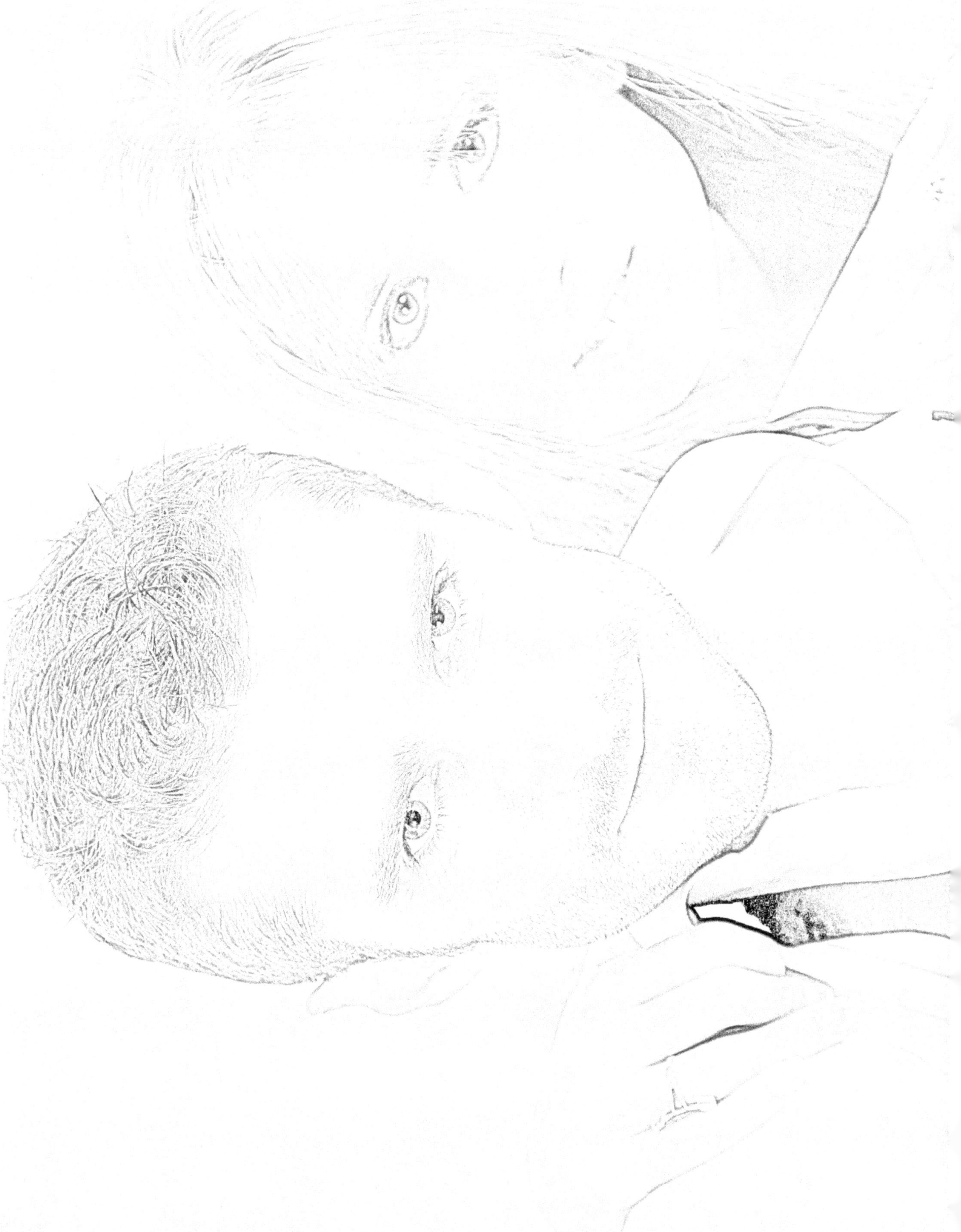

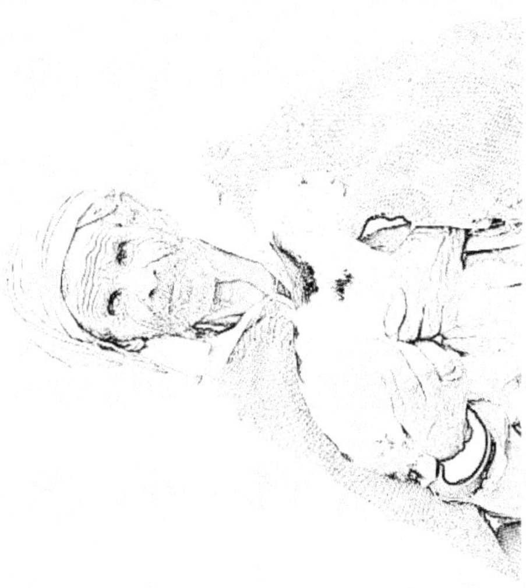
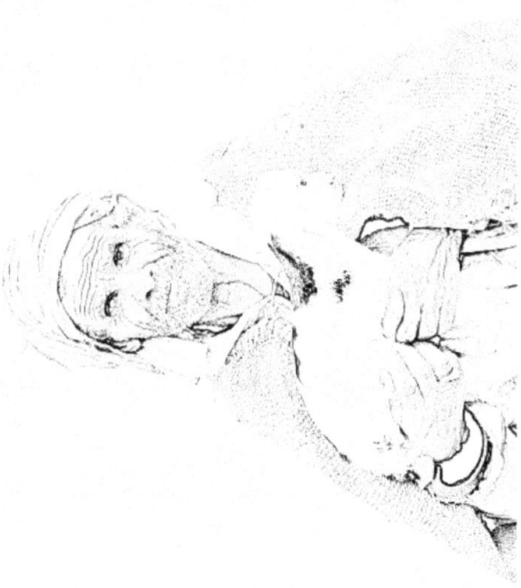
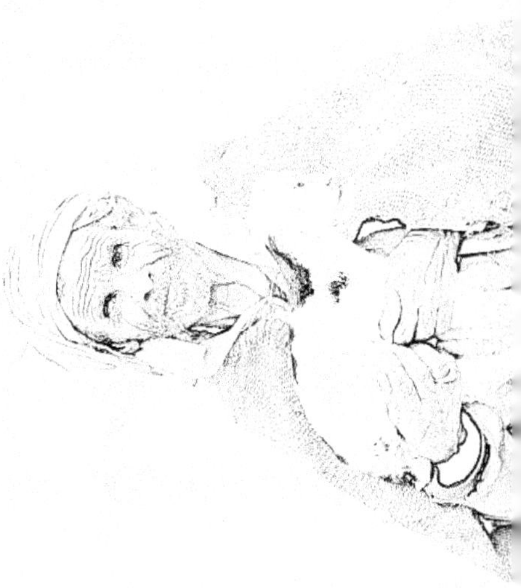

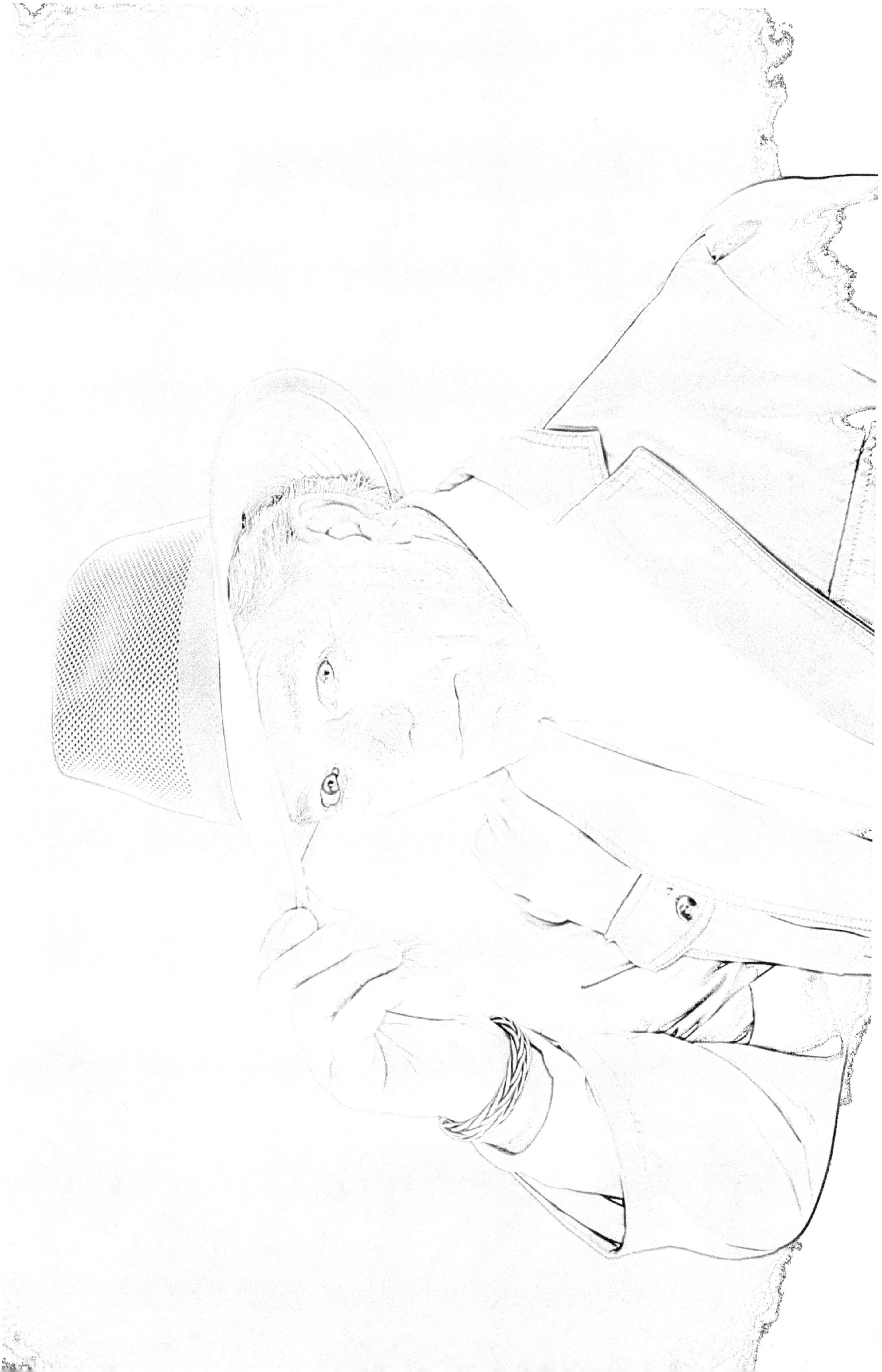

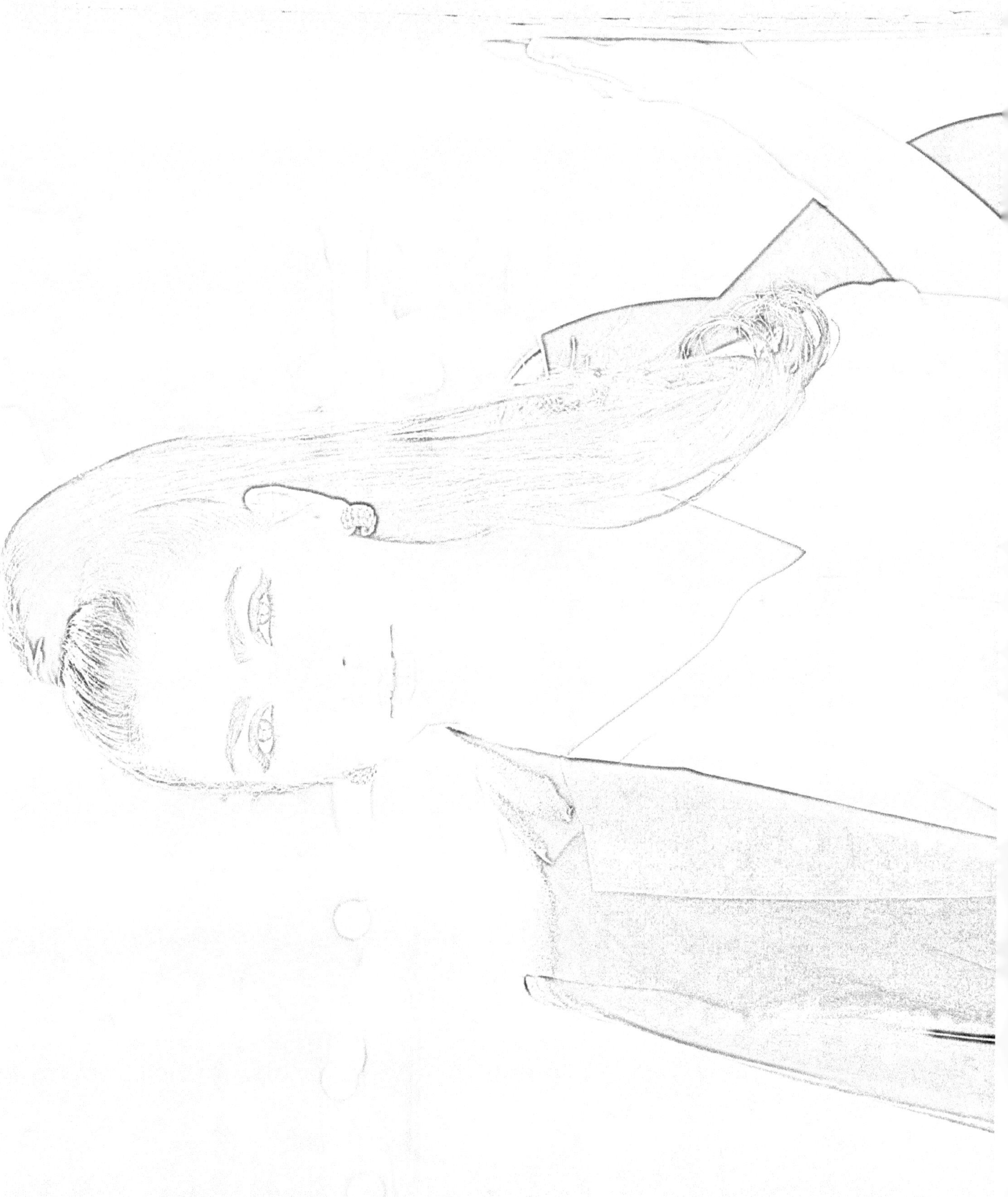

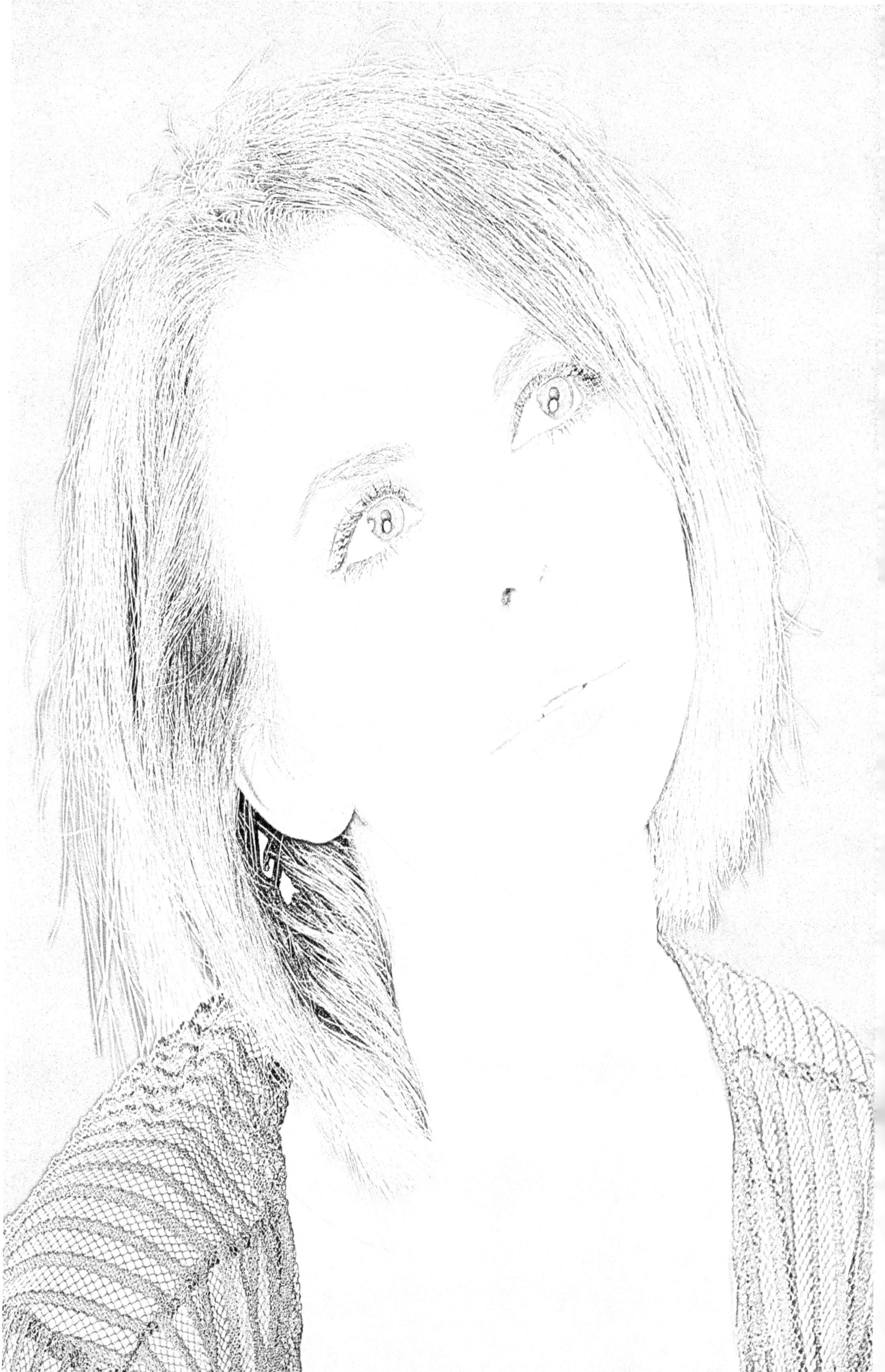

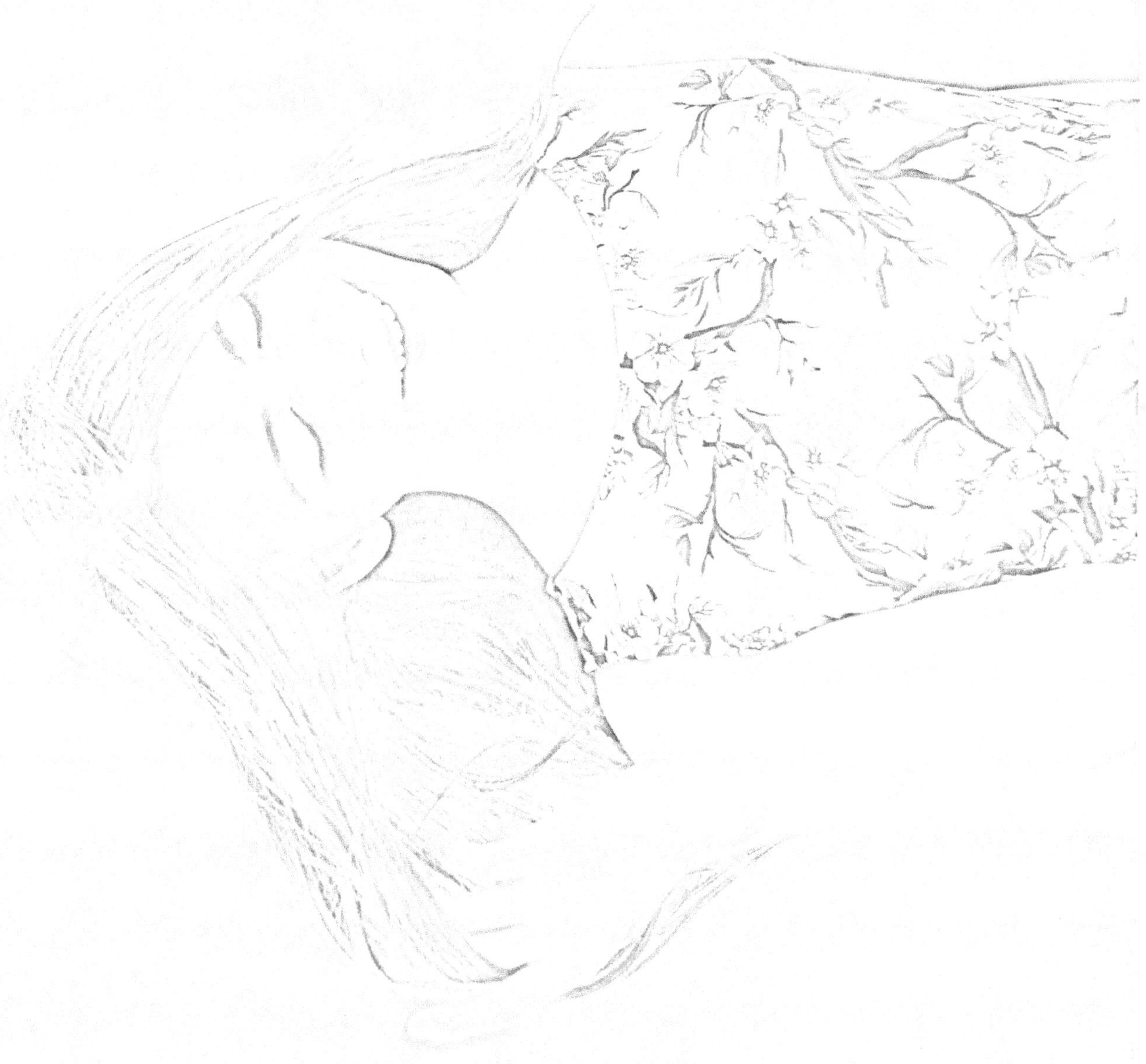

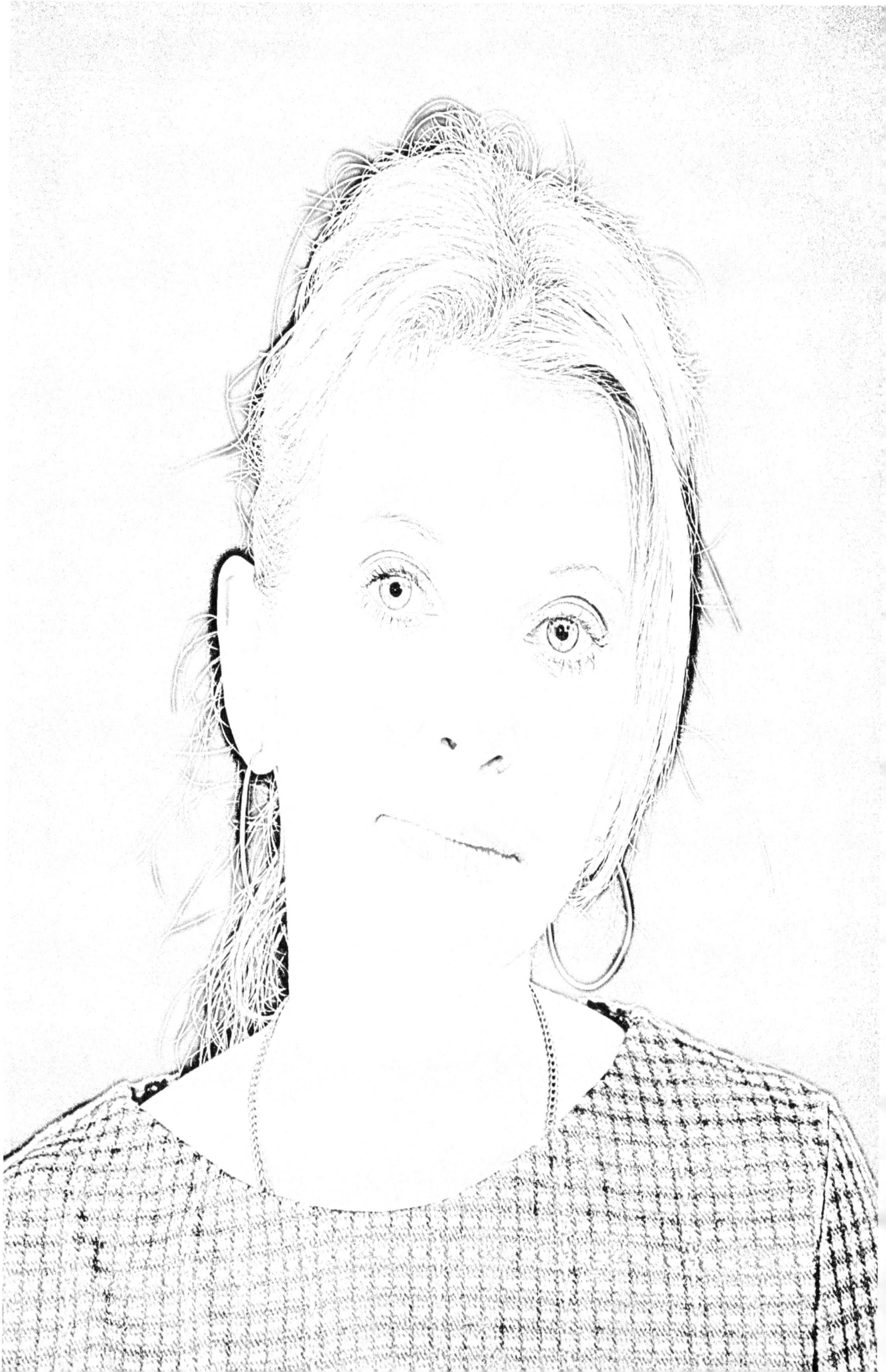

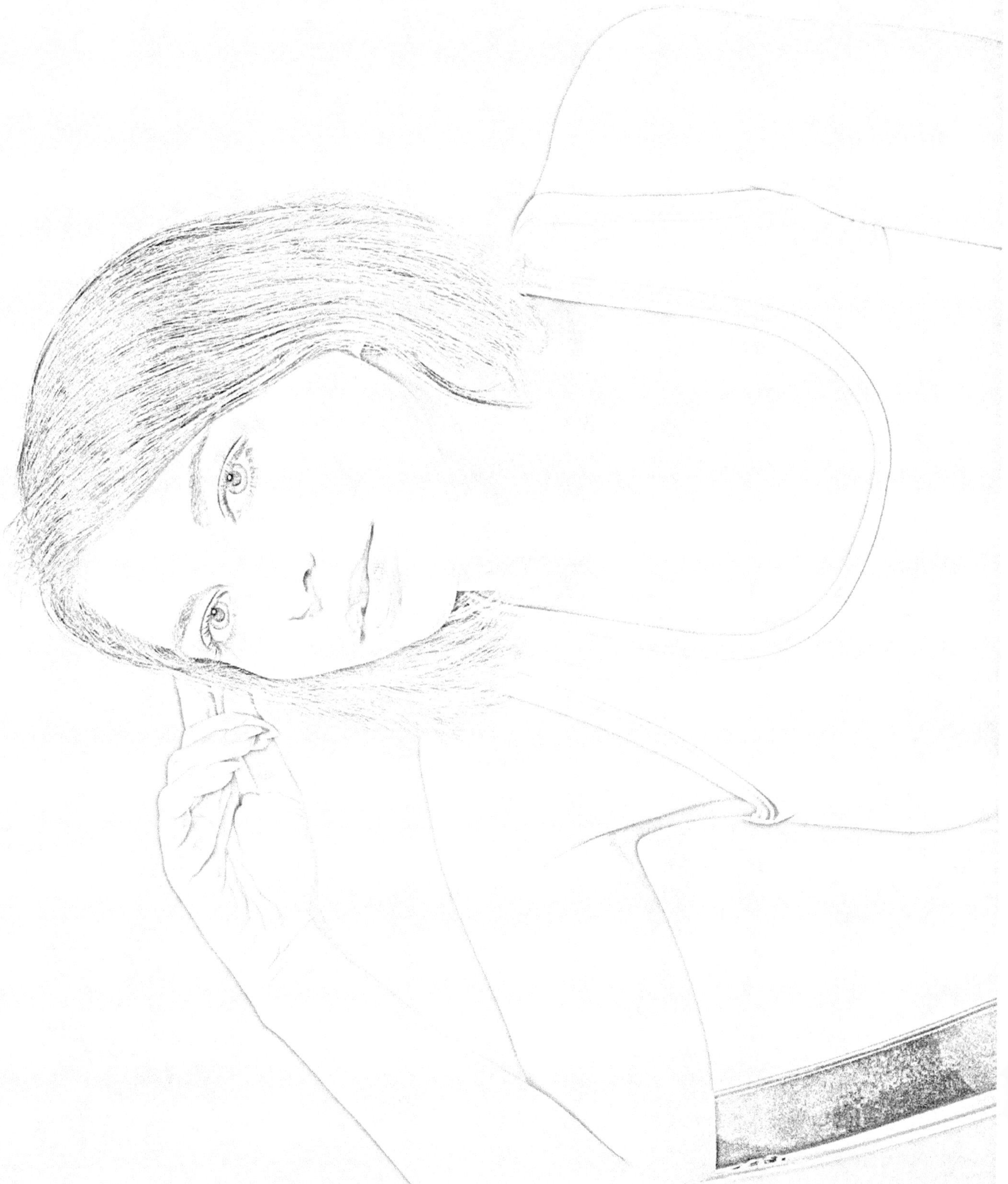

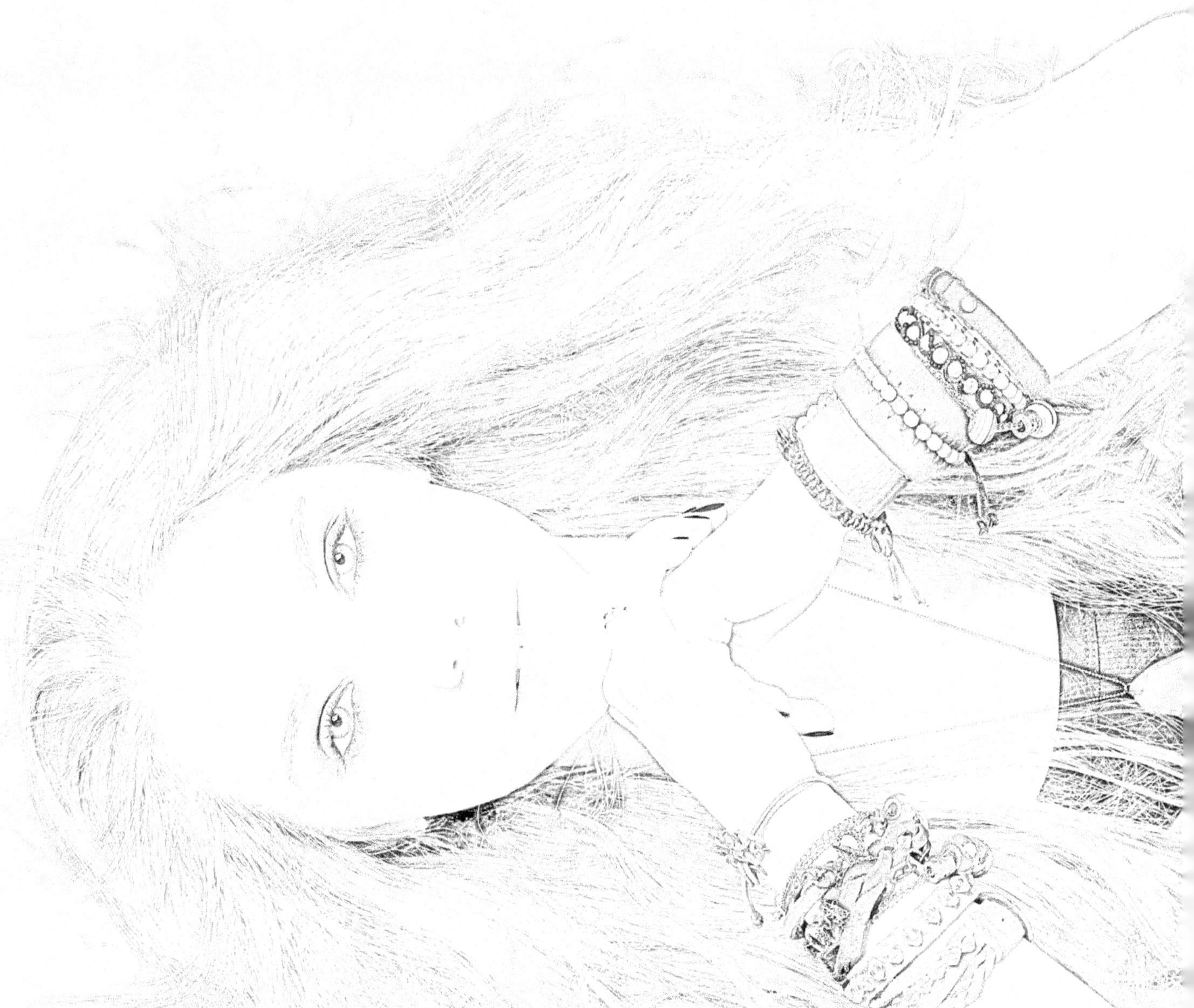

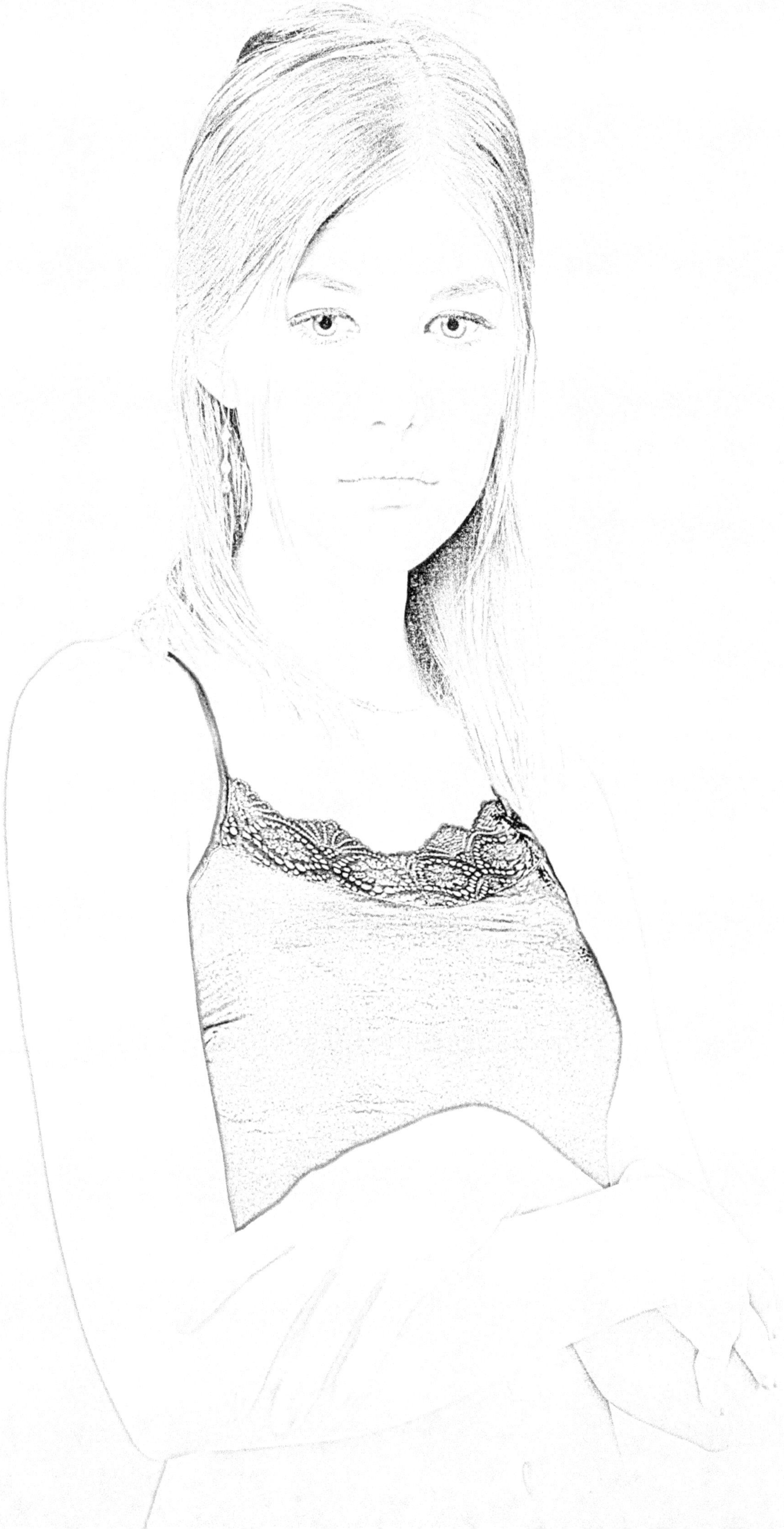

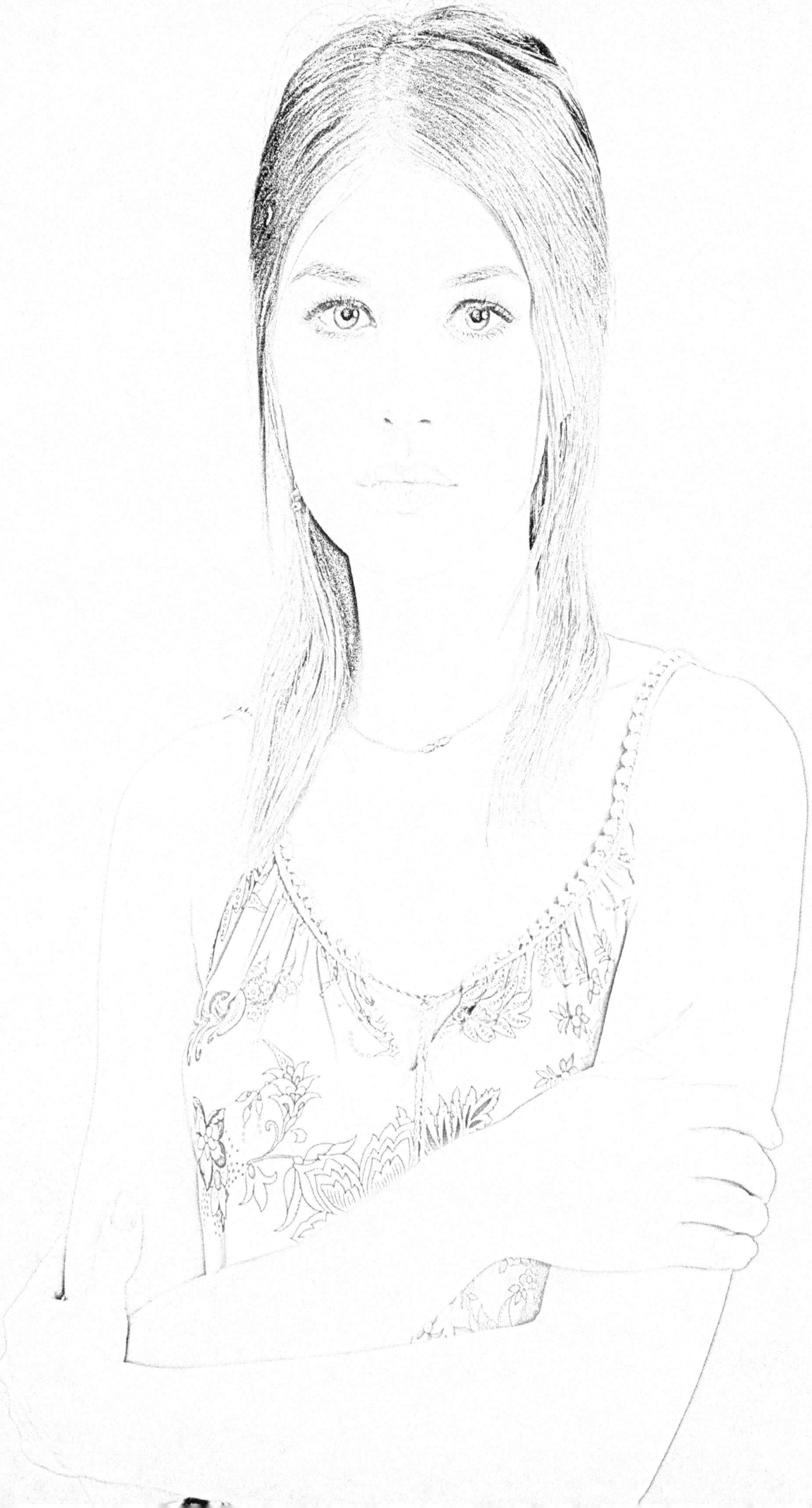

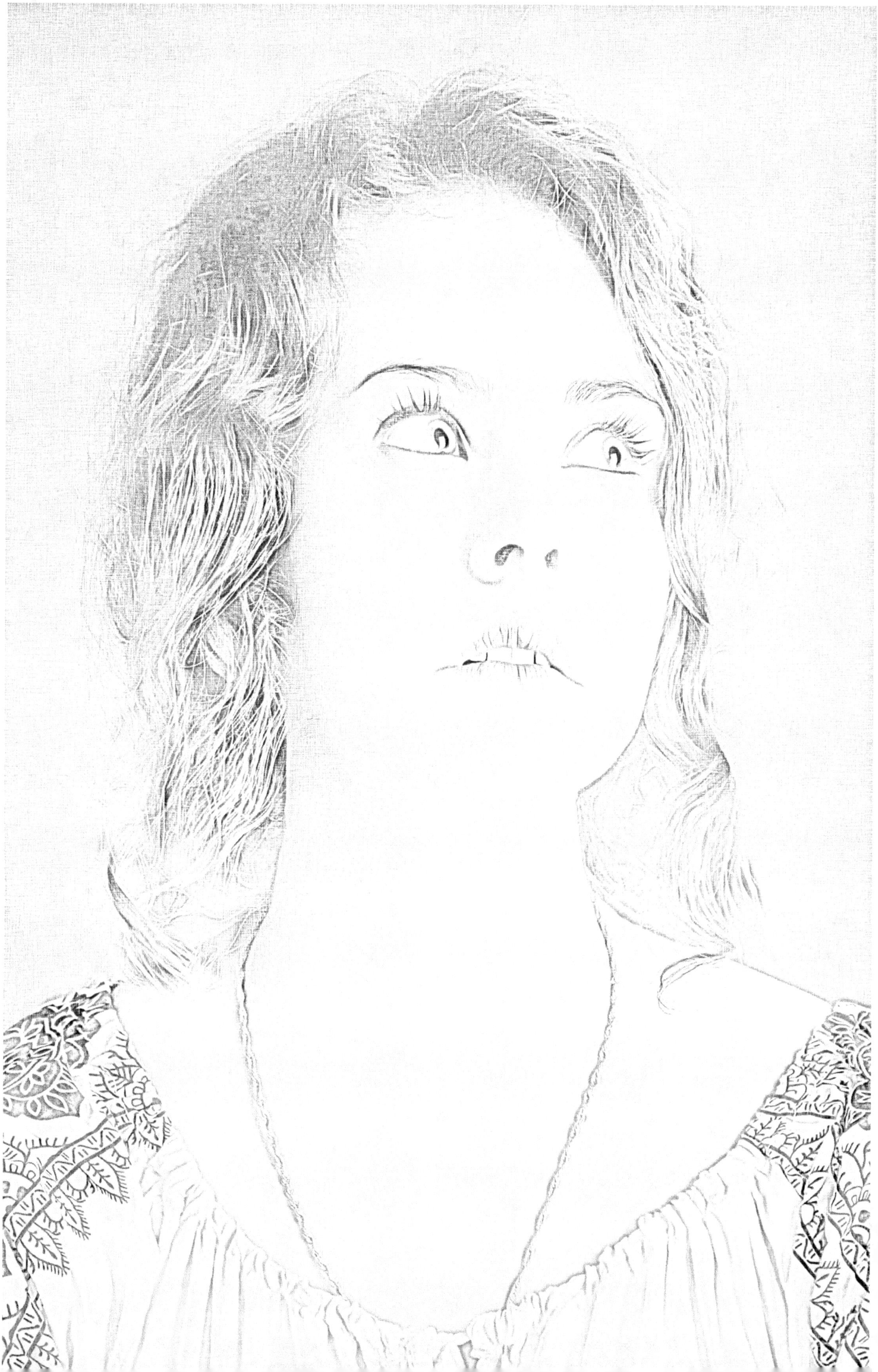

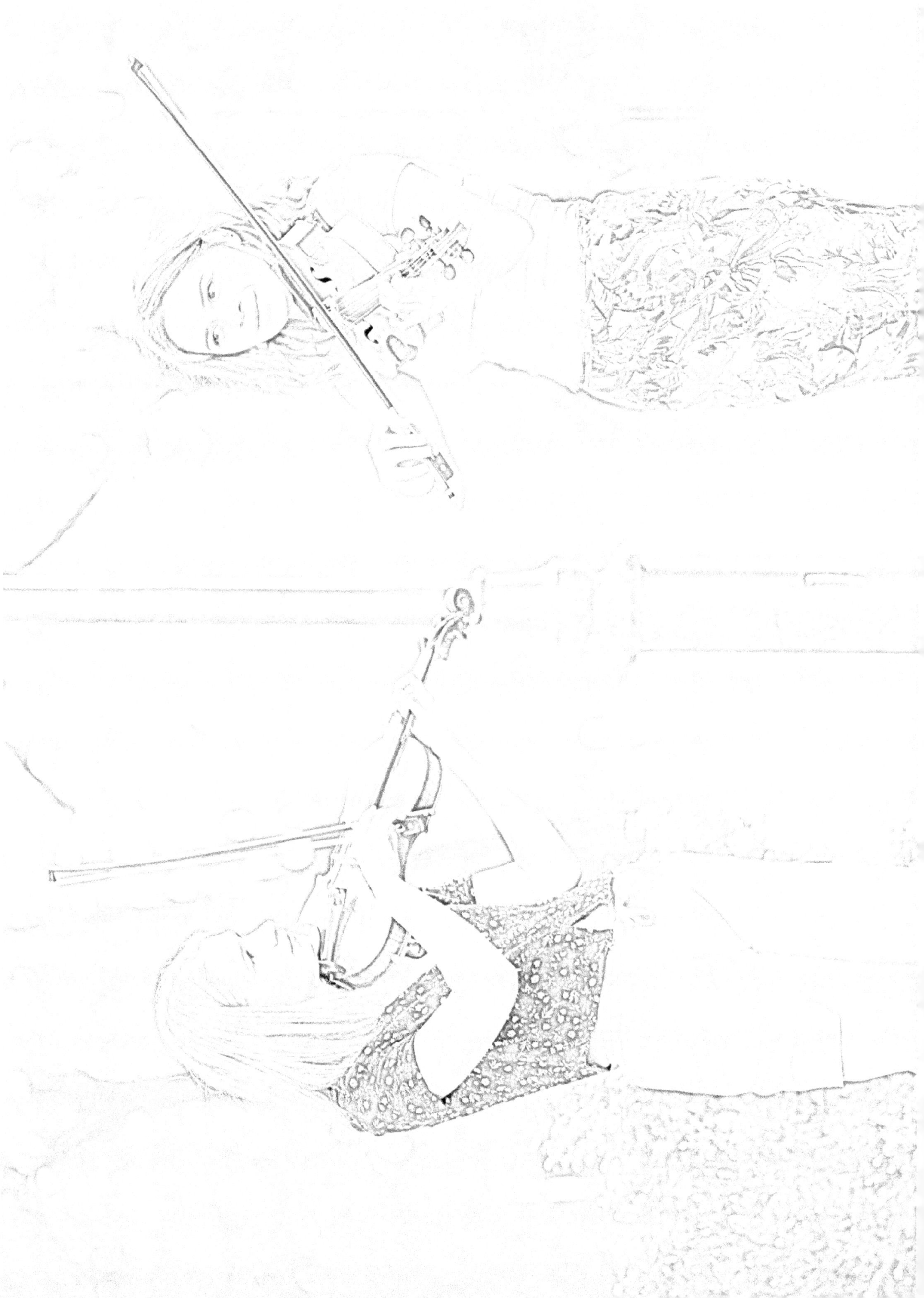

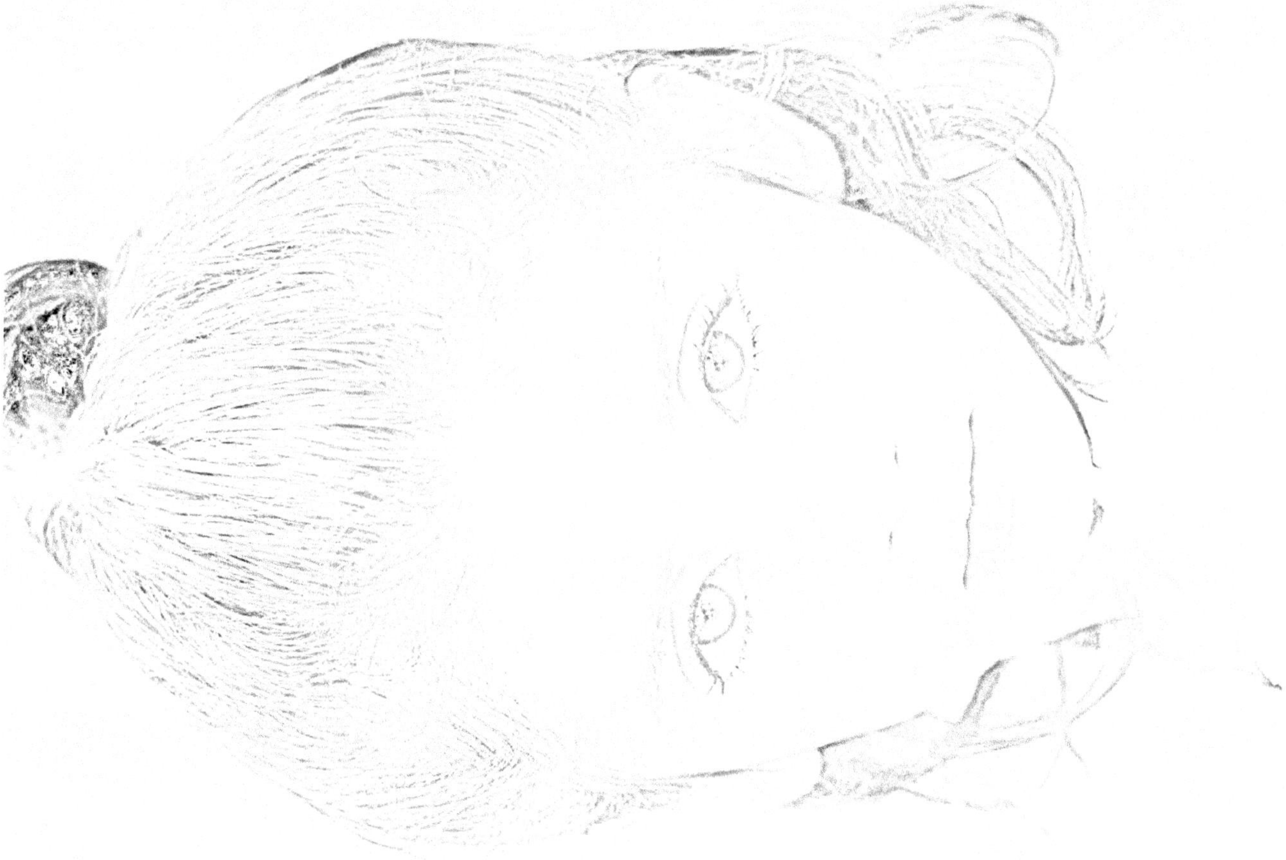

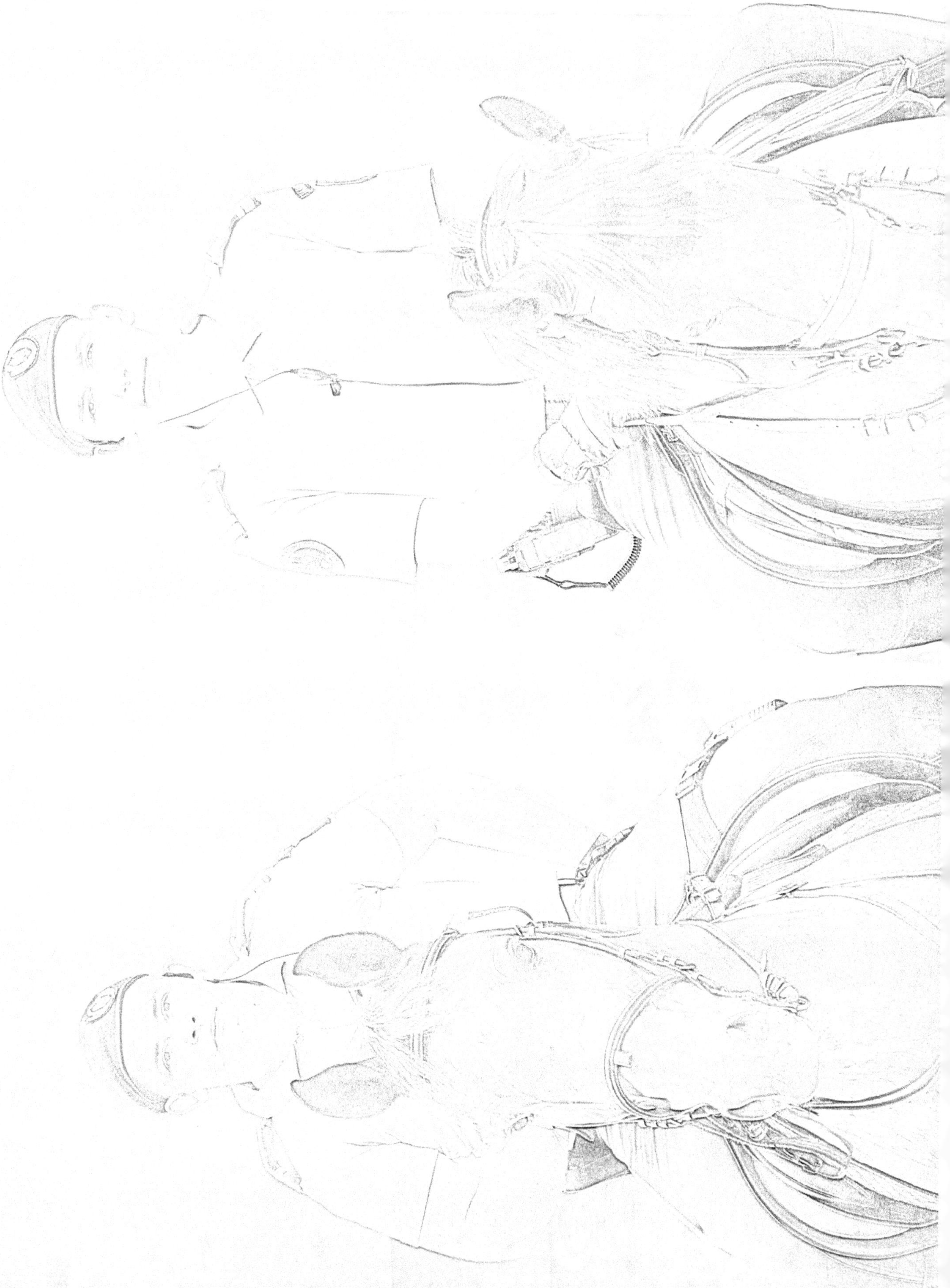

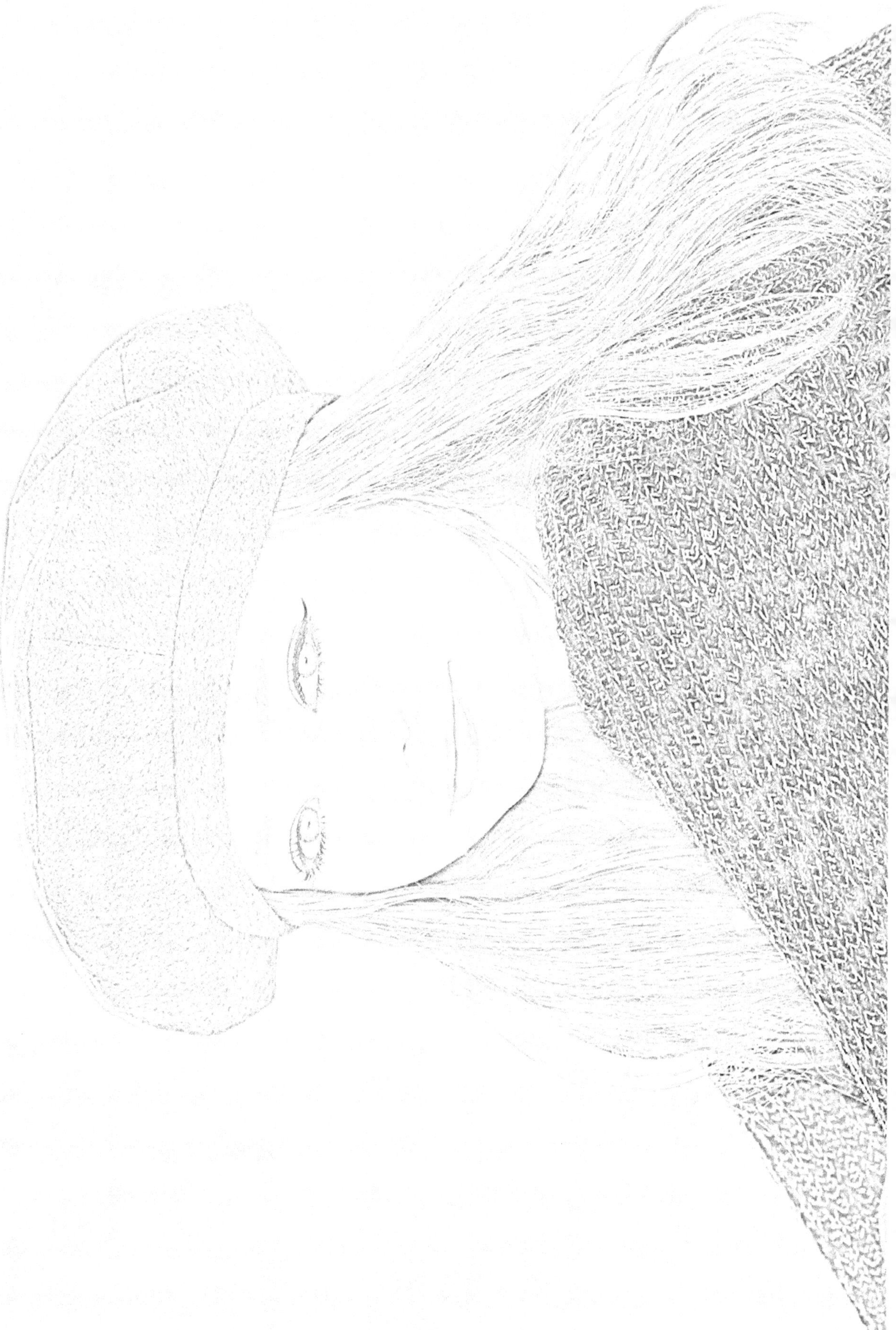

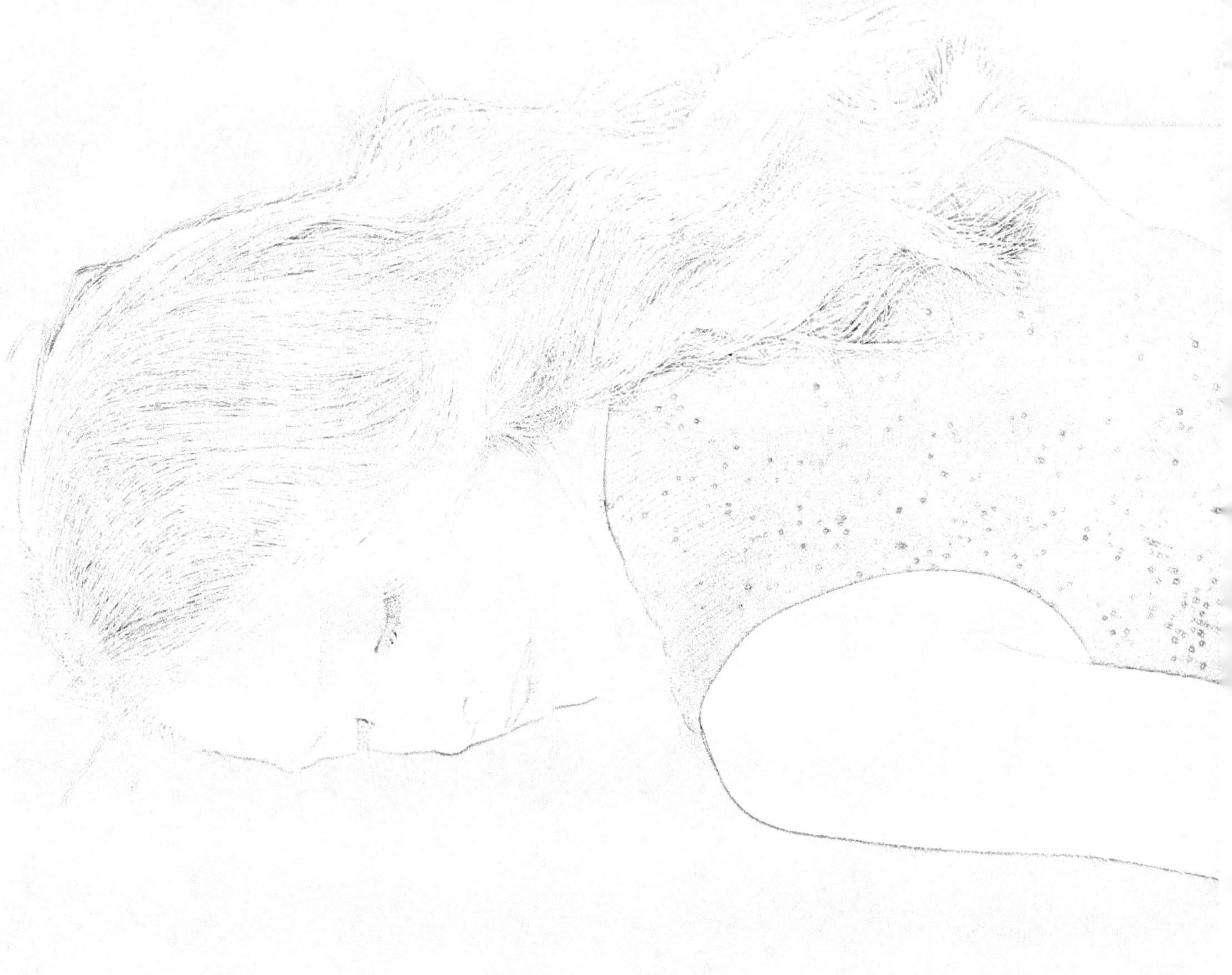

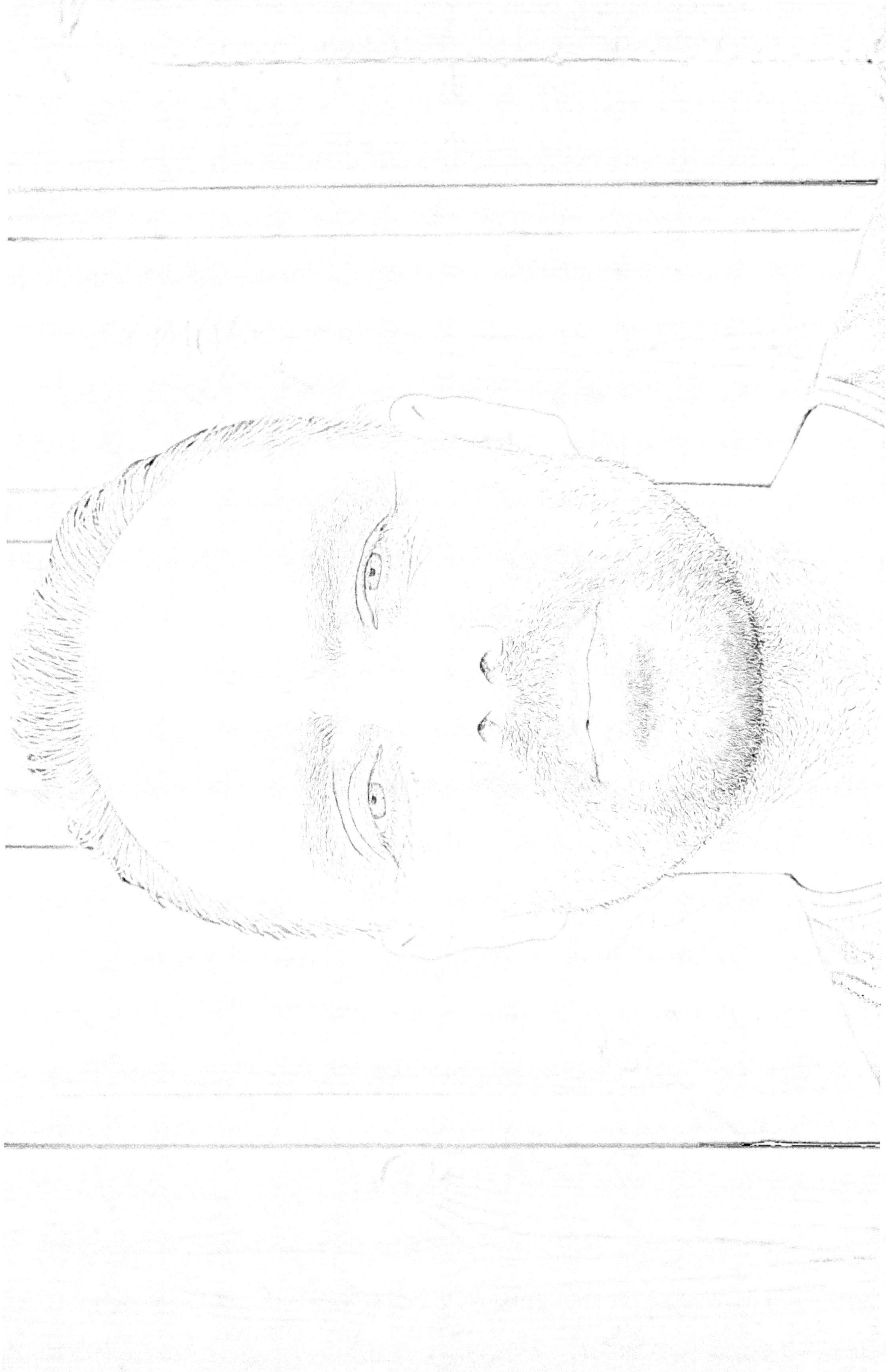

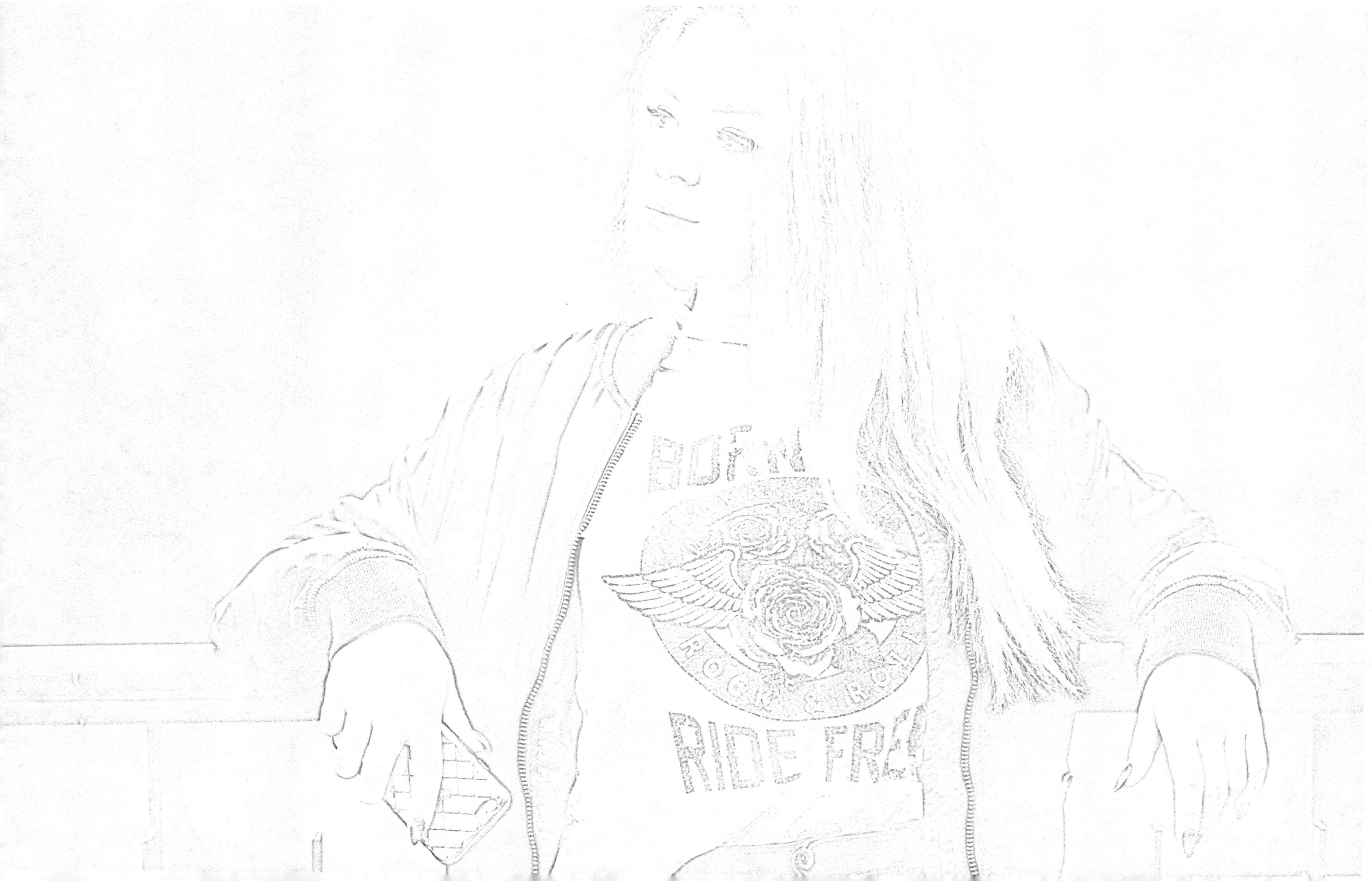

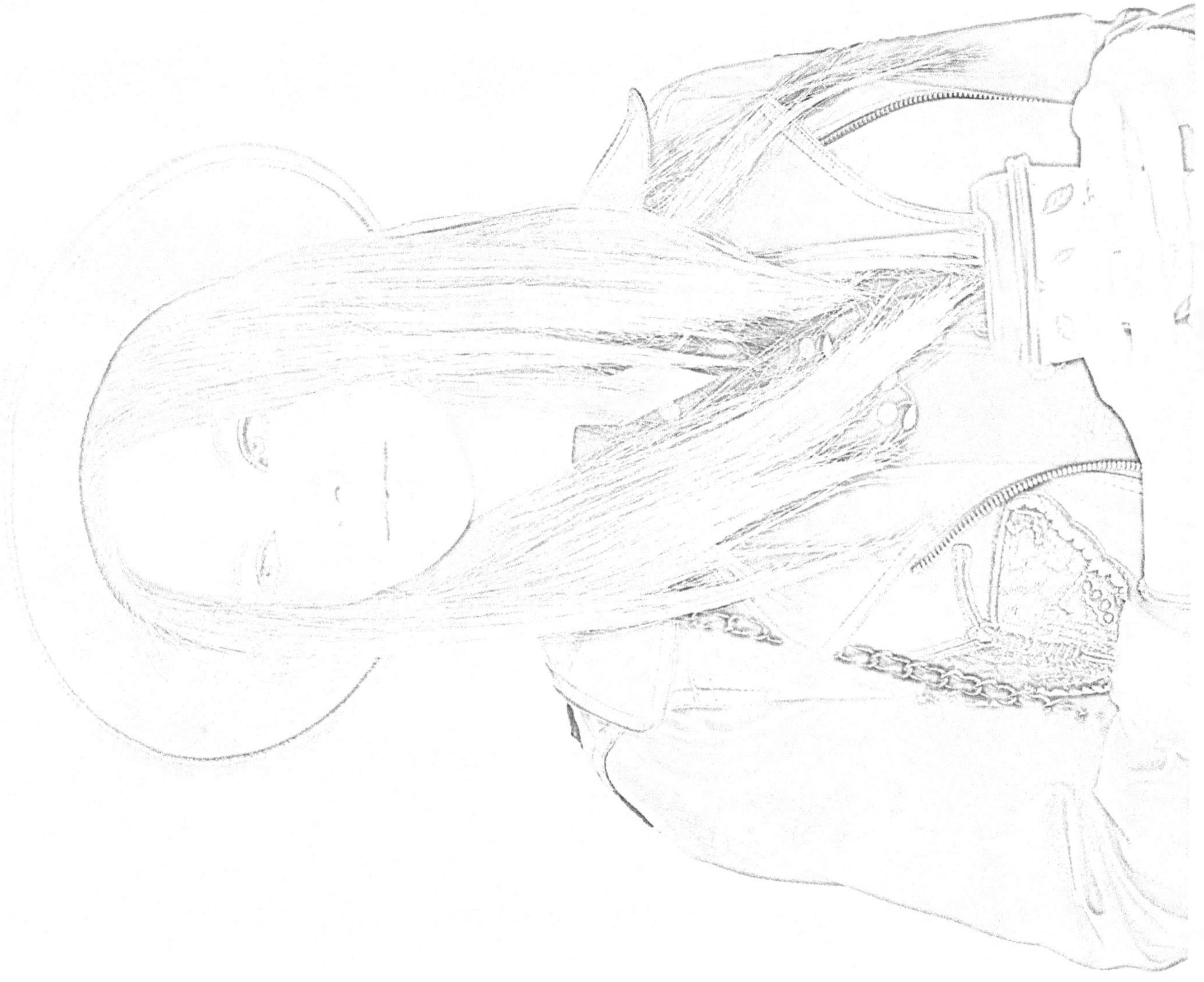

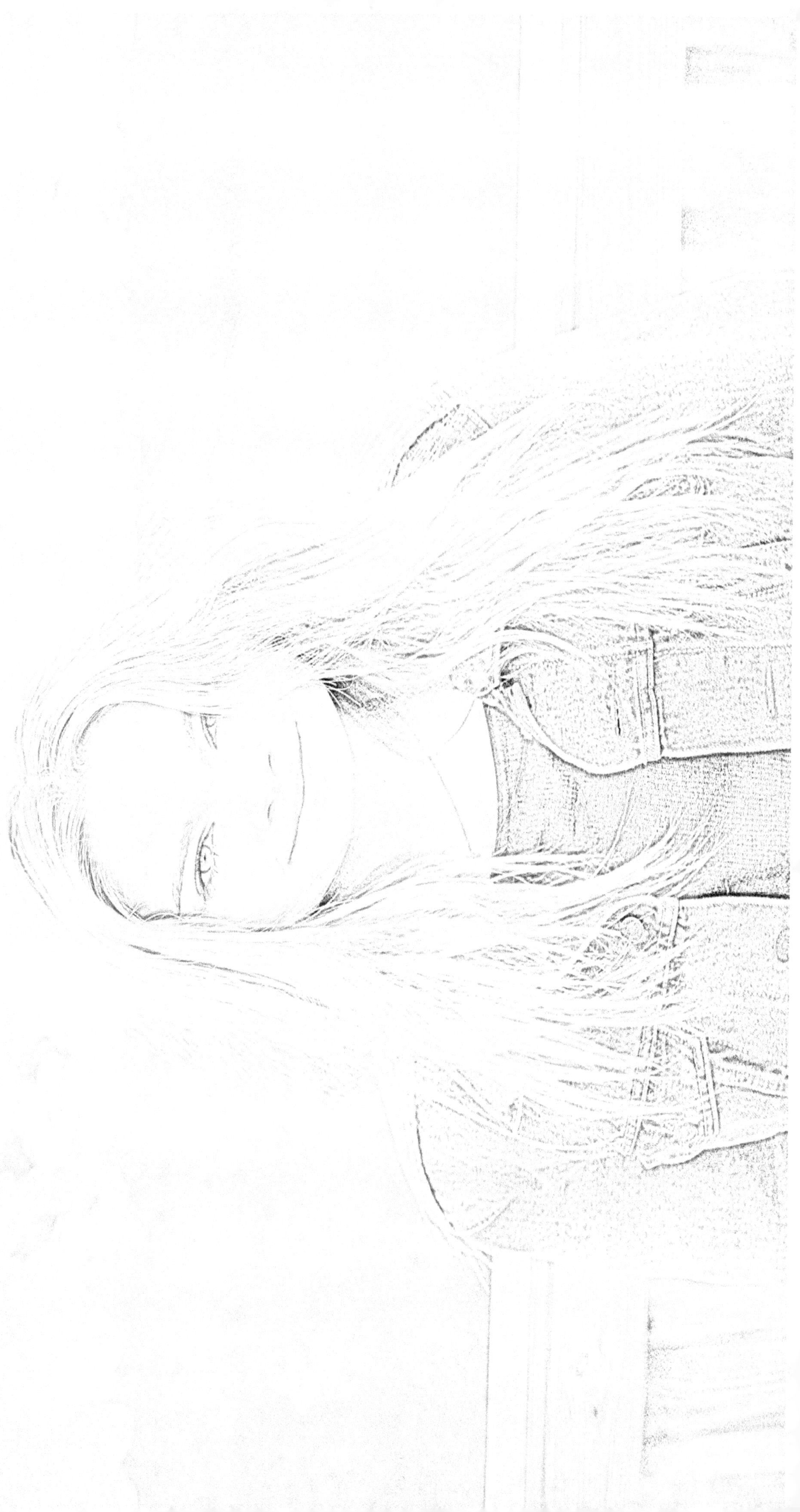

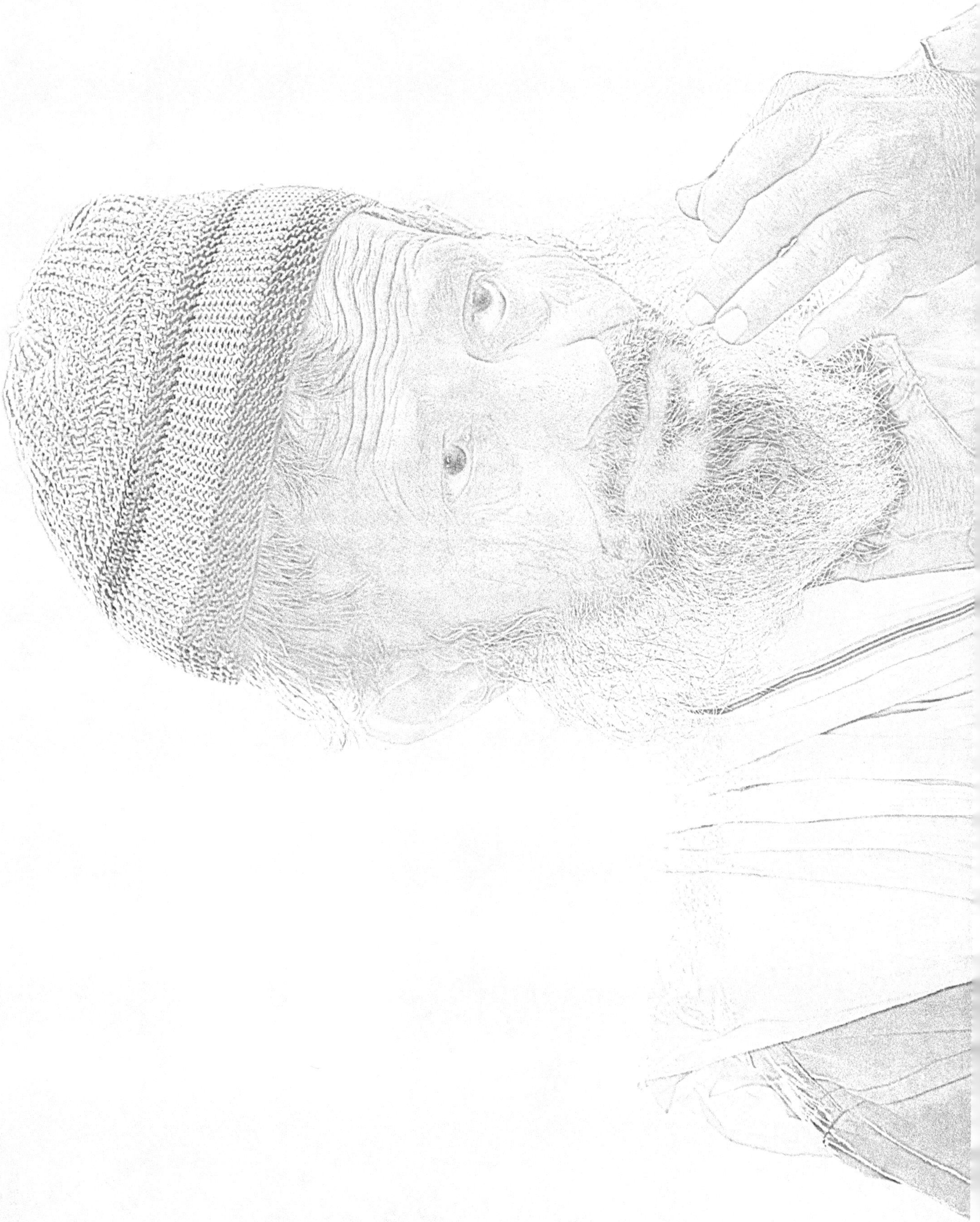

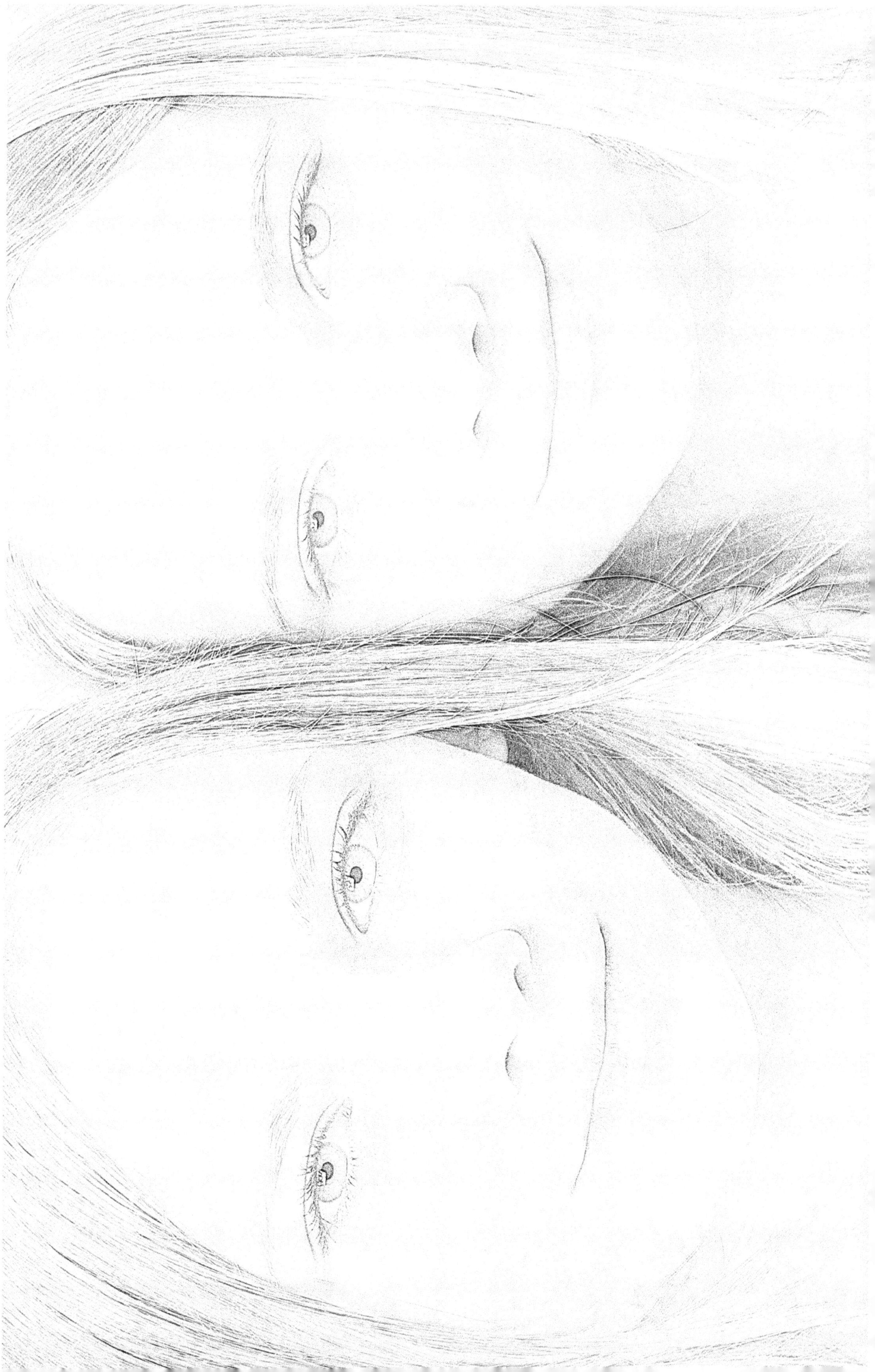

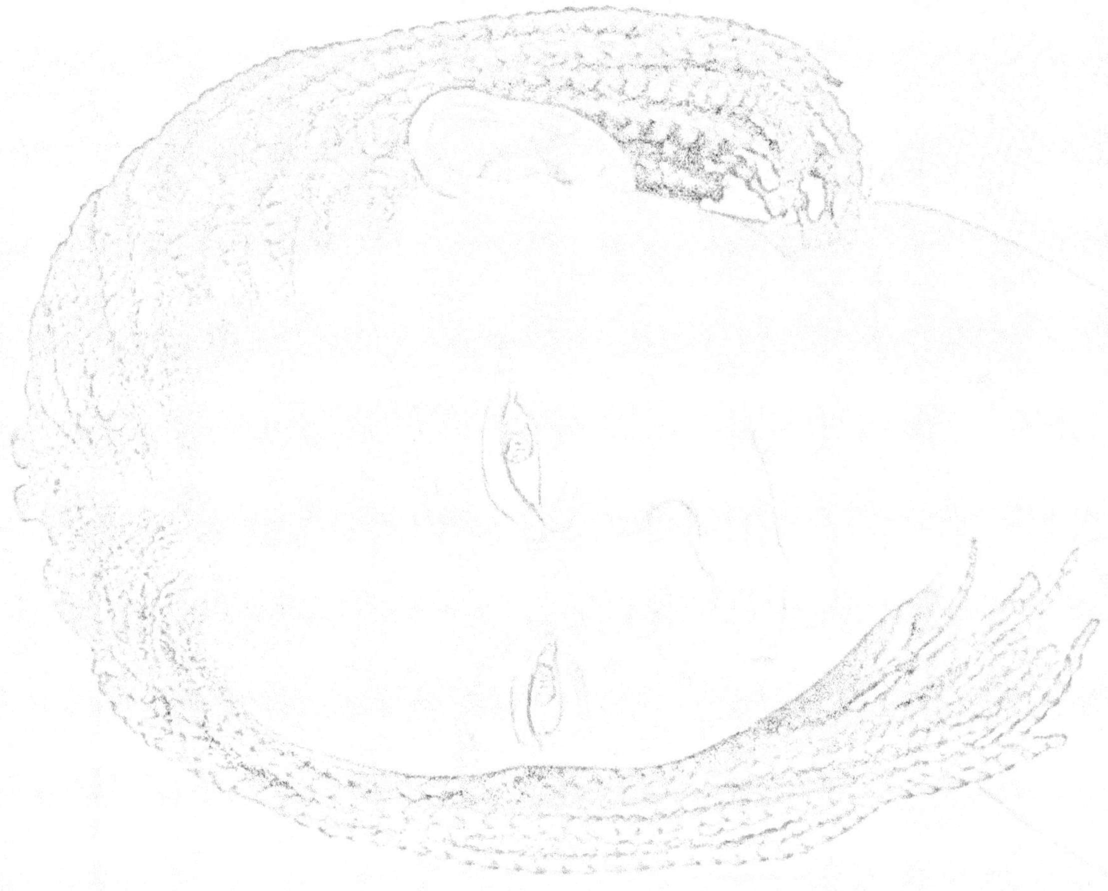

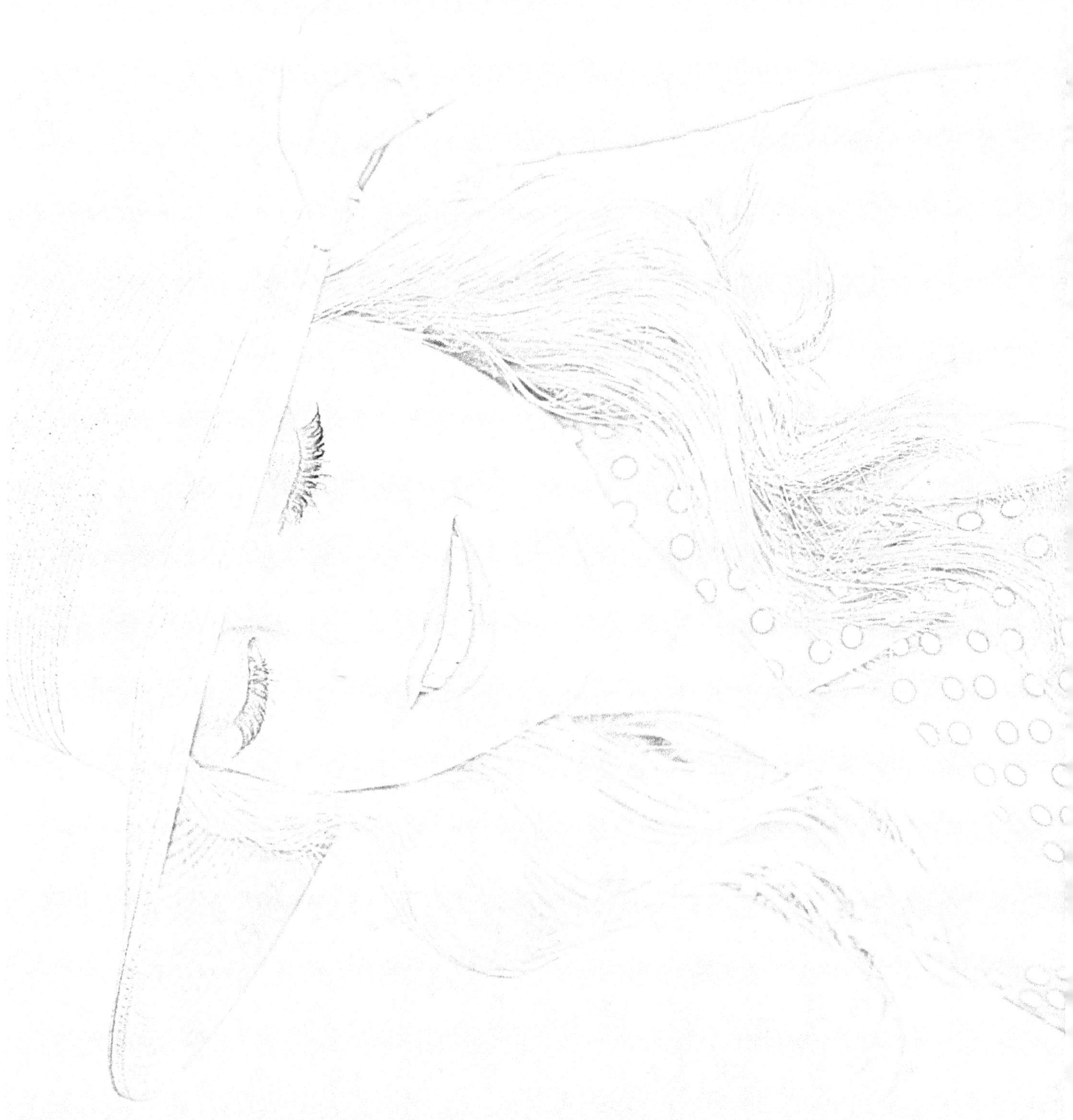

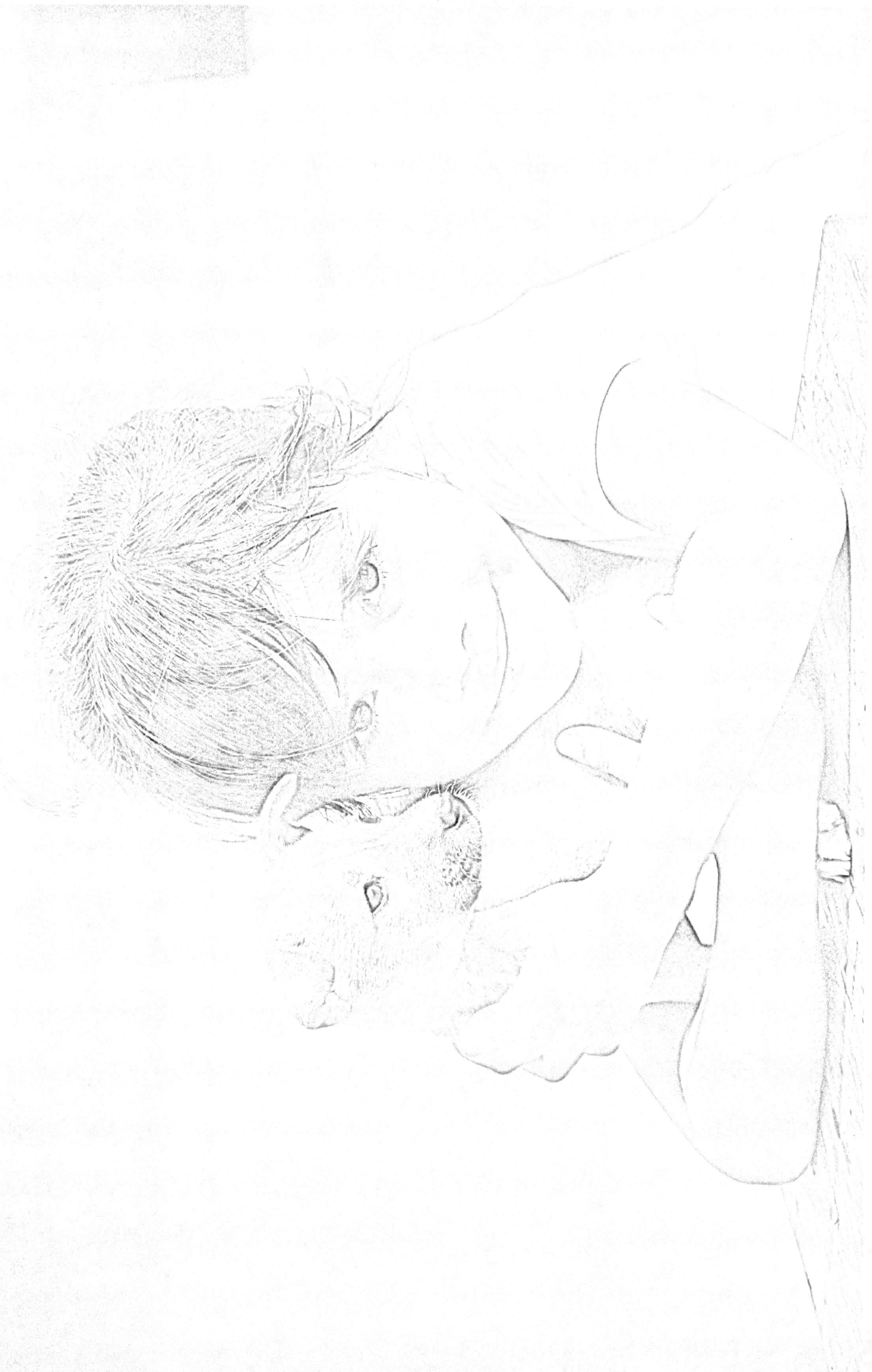

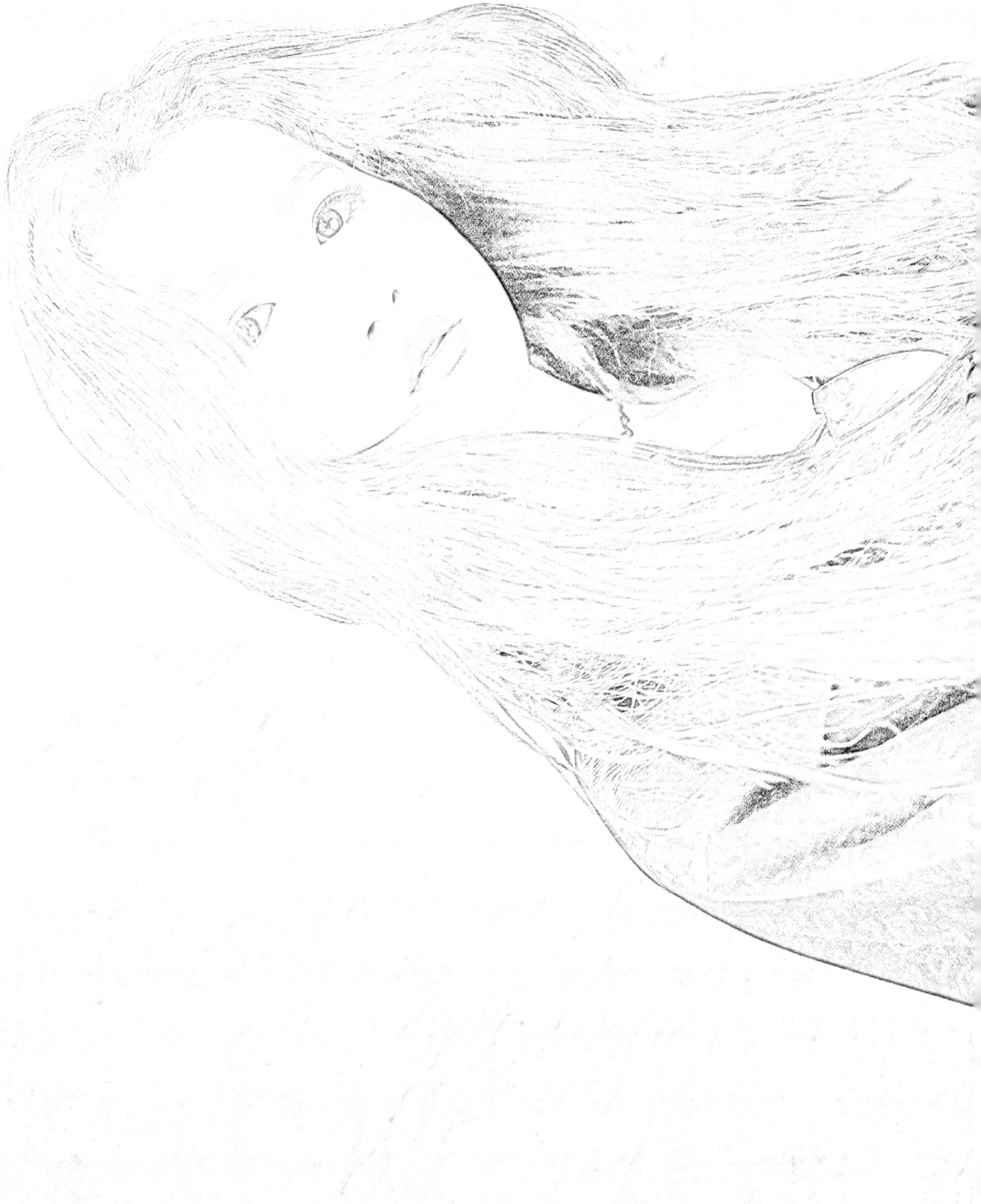

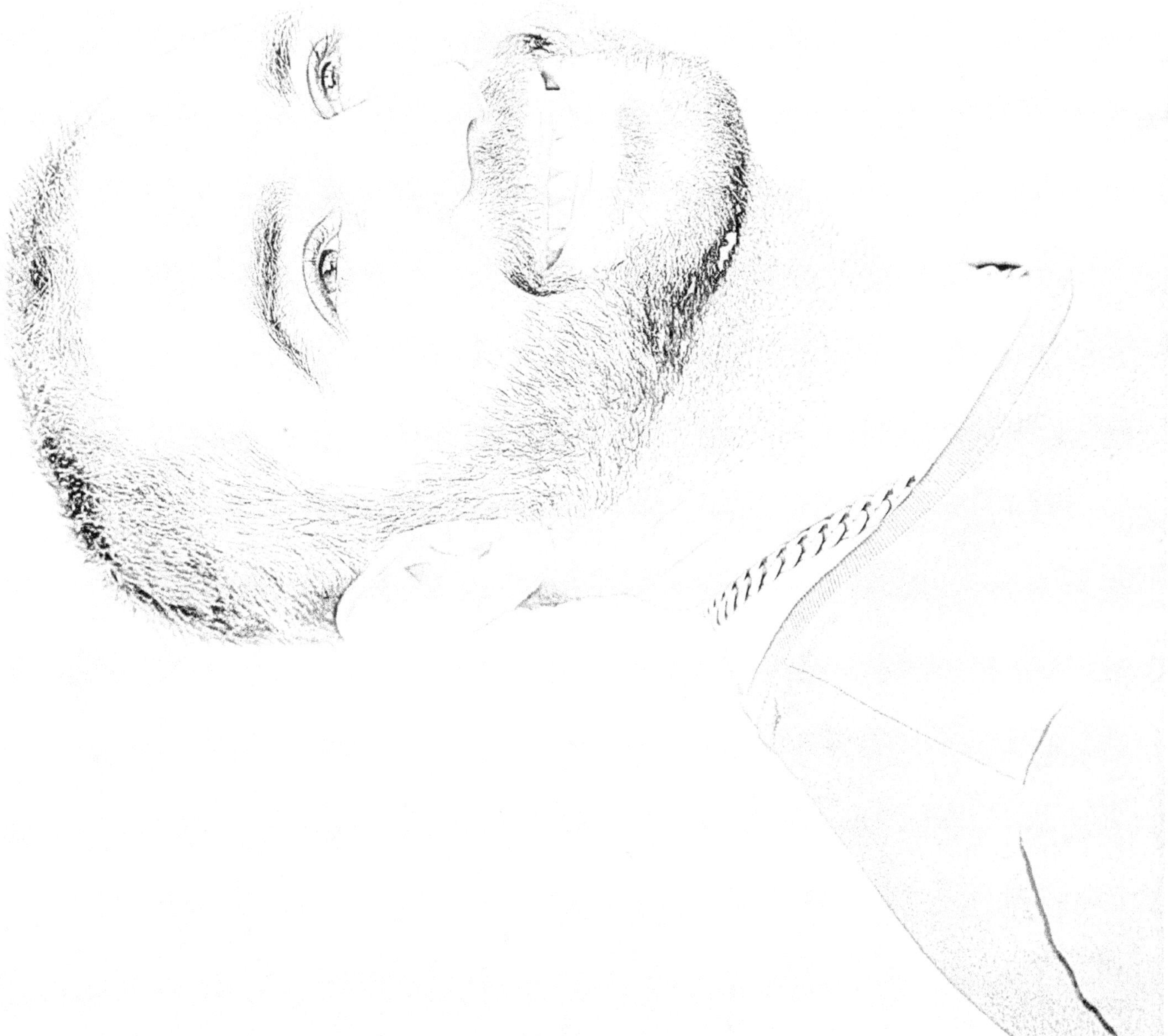

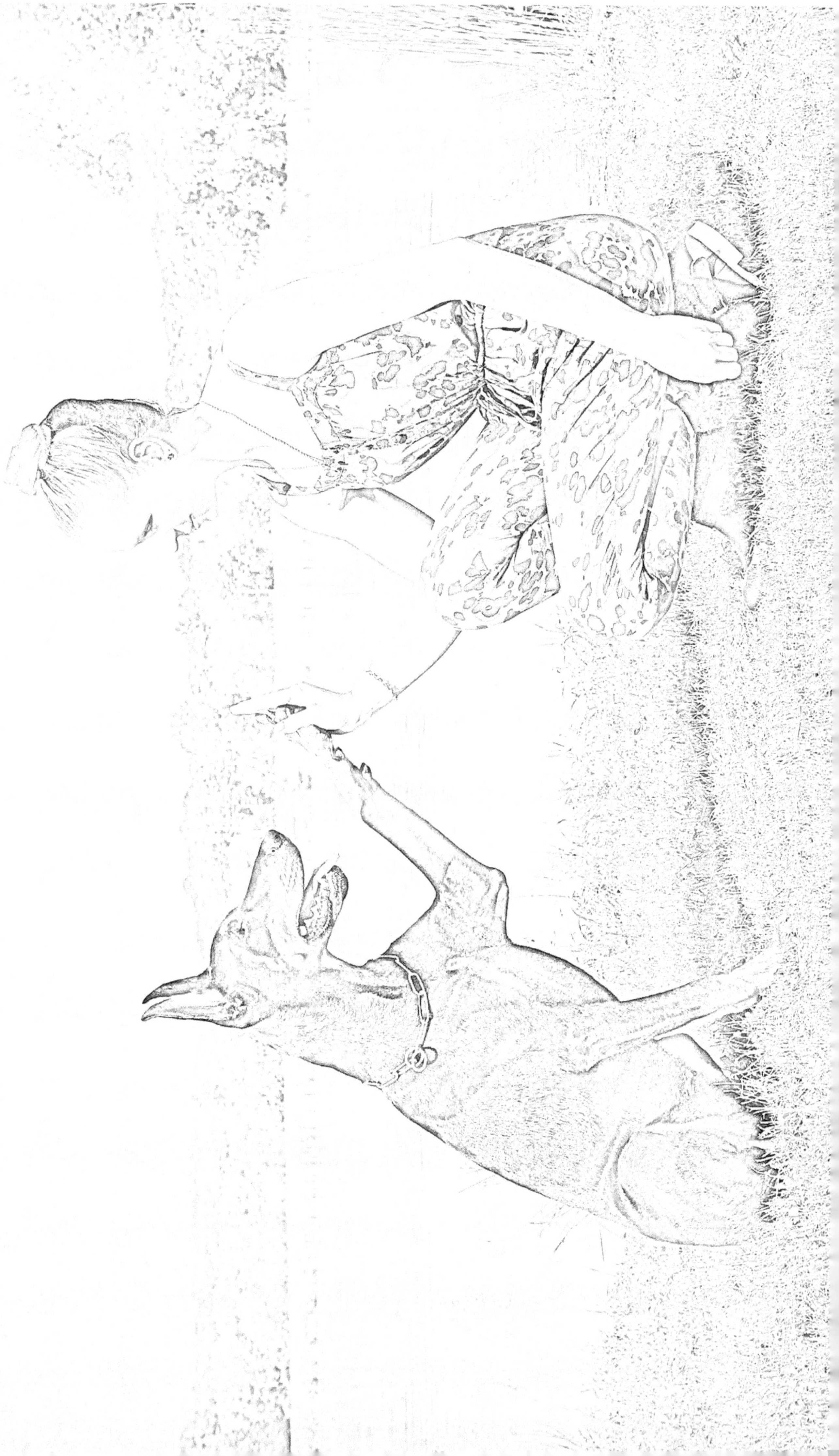

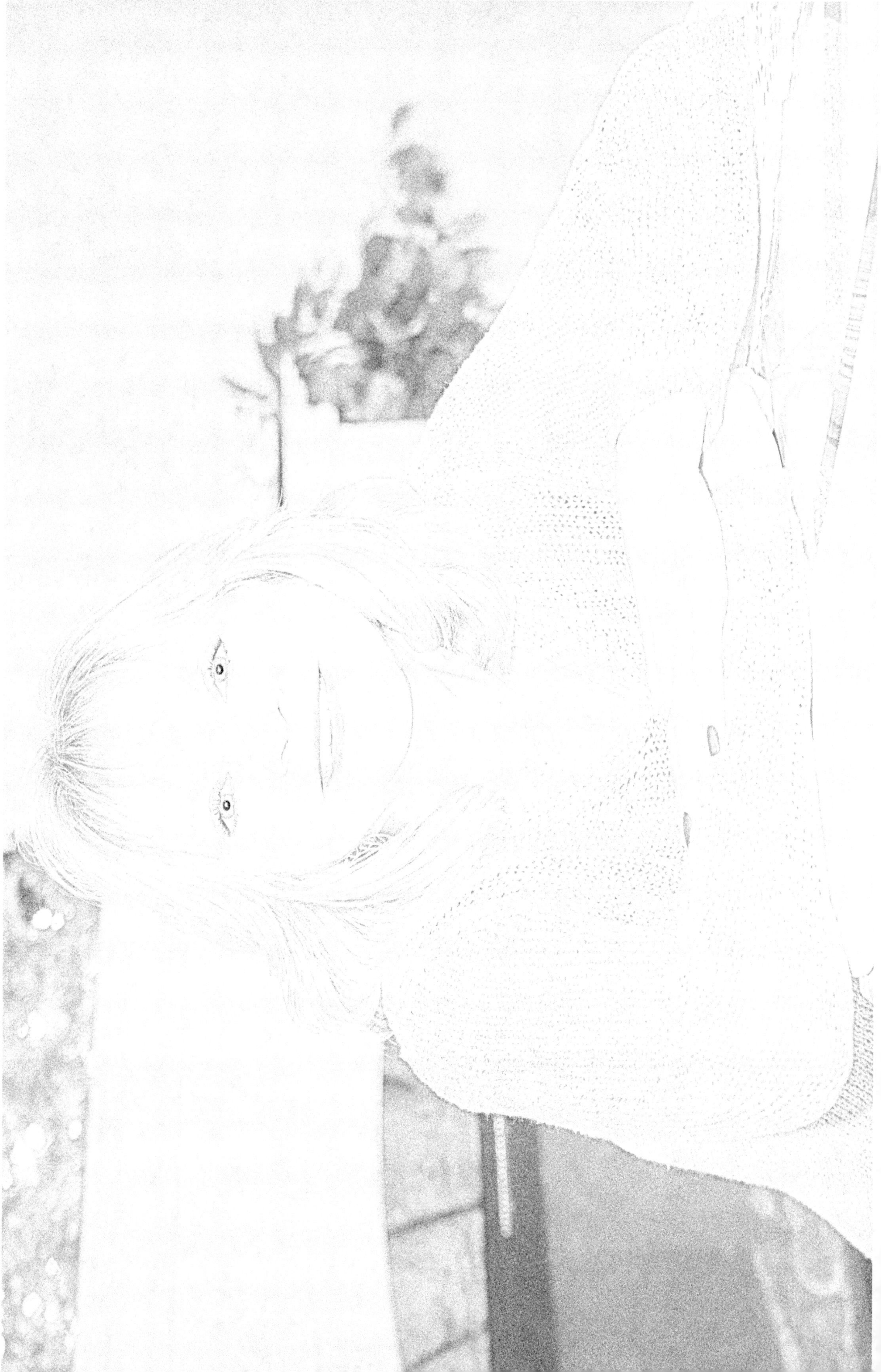

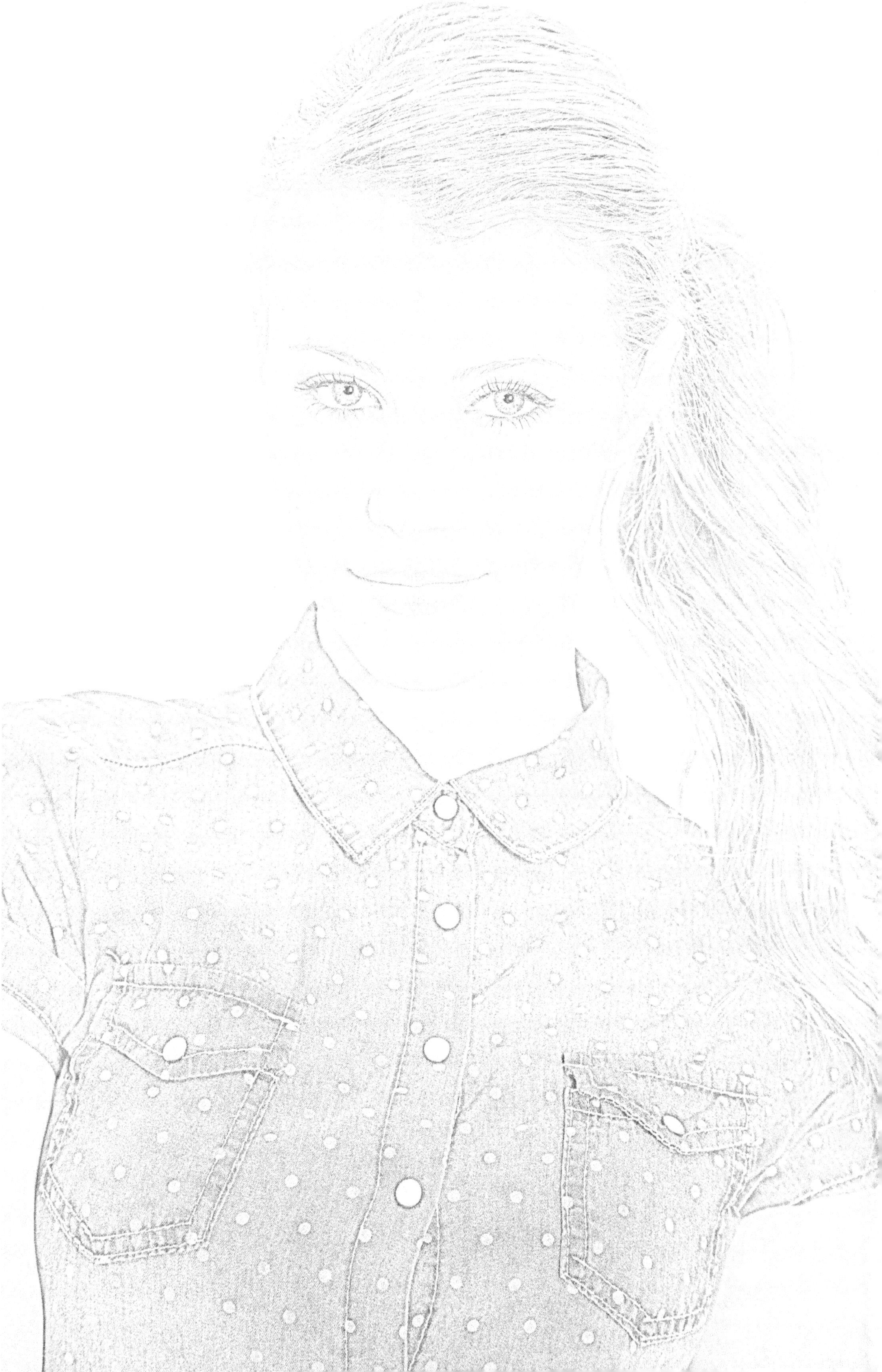

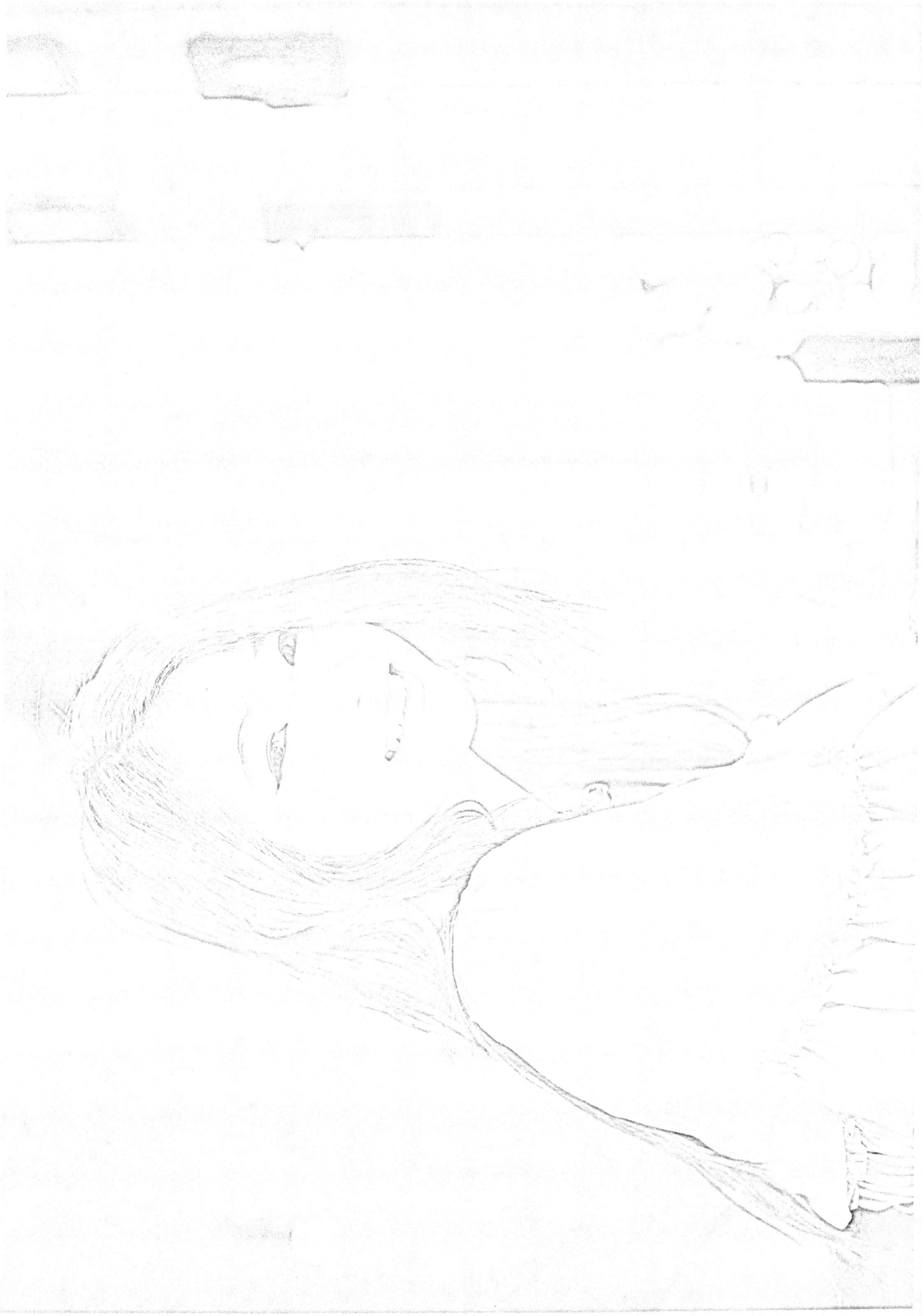

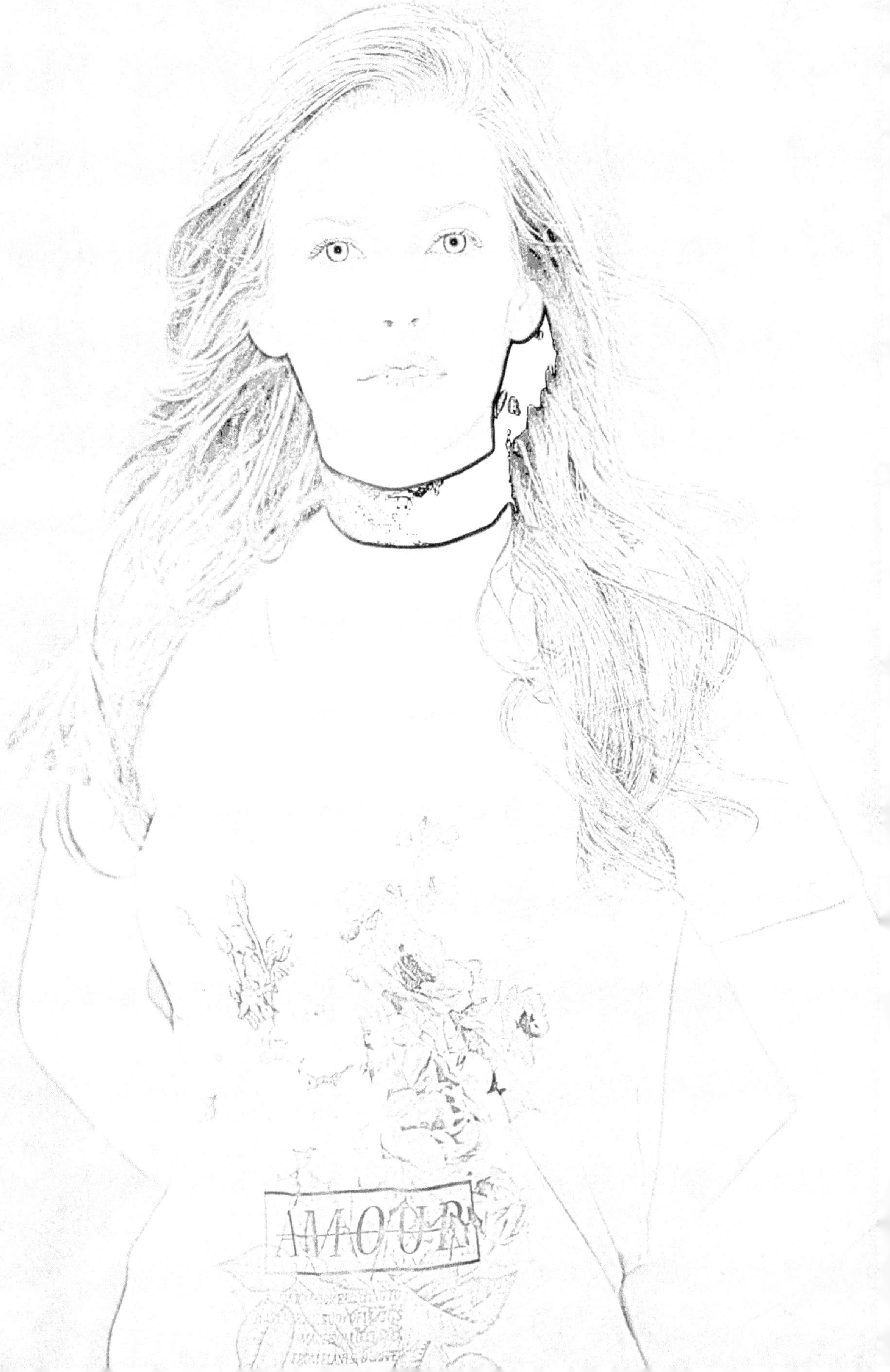
AMOUR

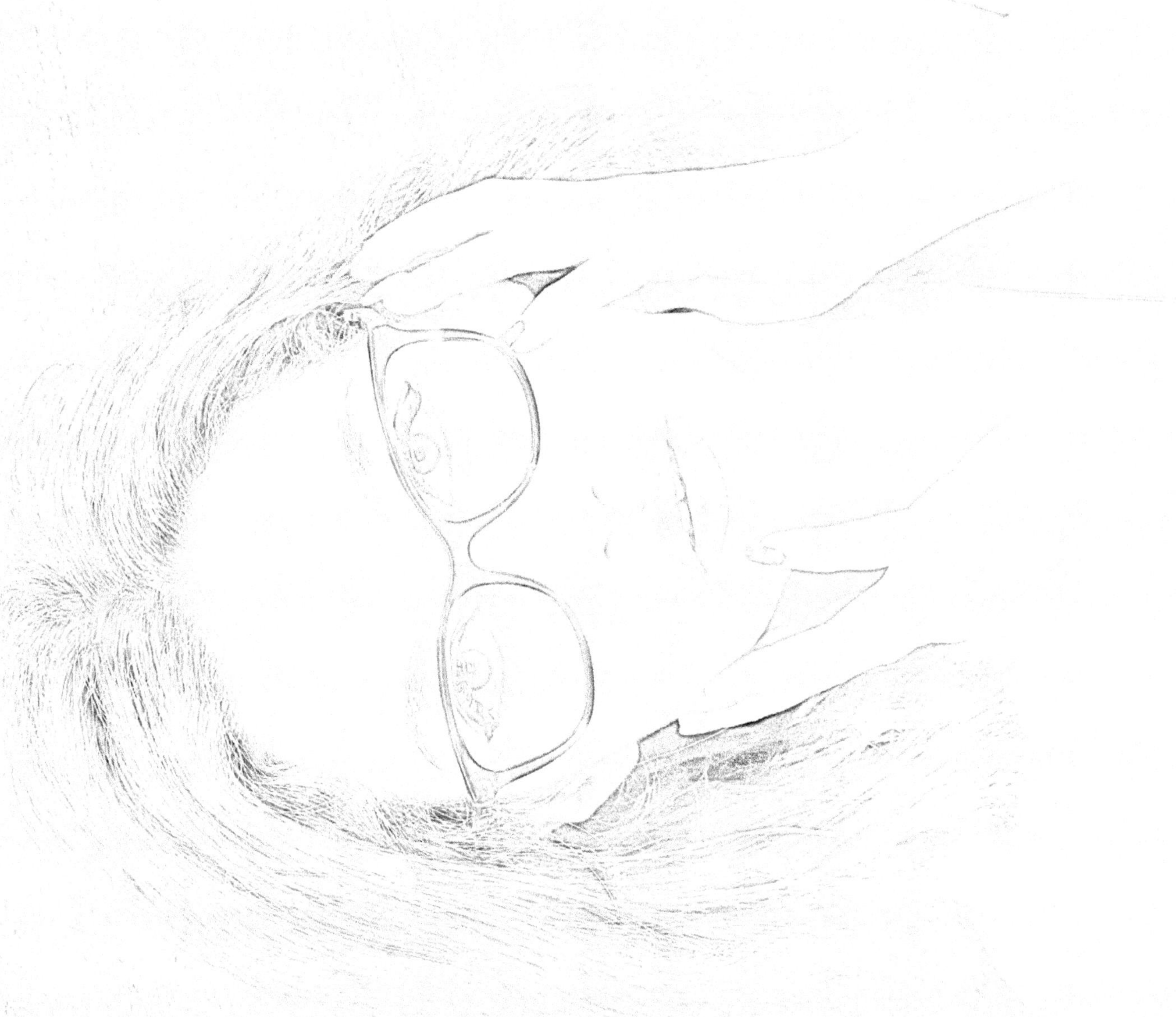

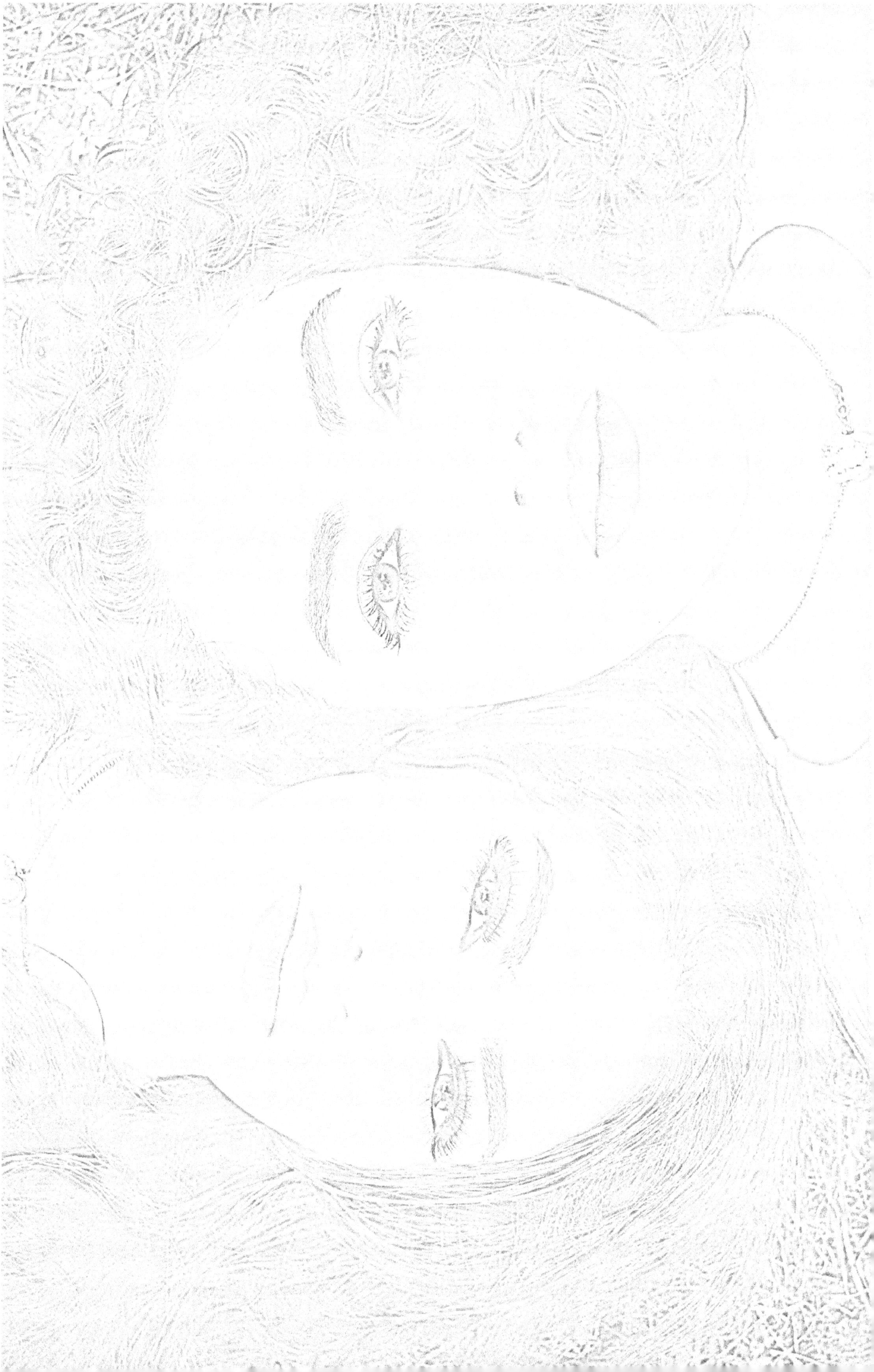

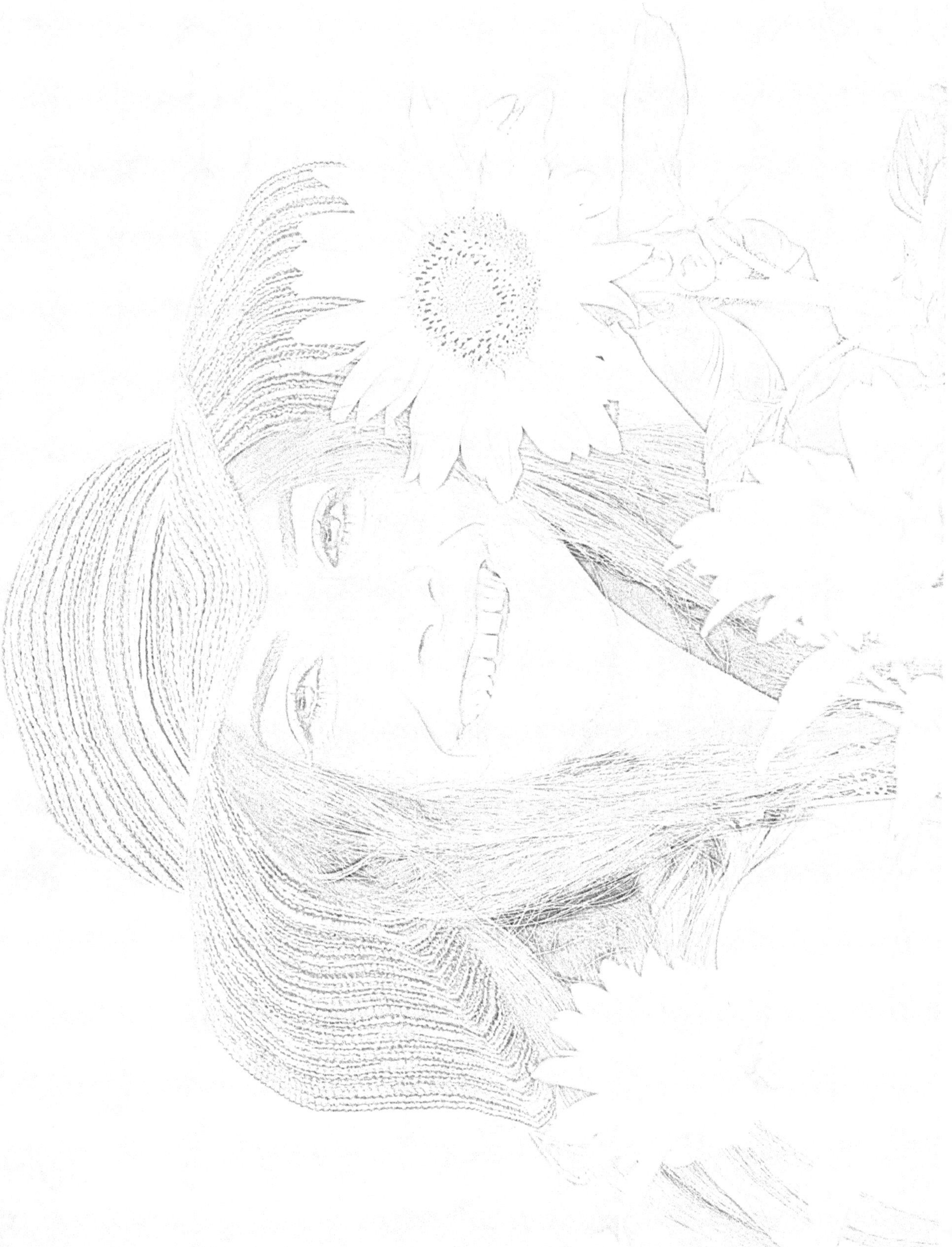

www.ingramcontent.com/pod-product-compliance
Lightning Source LLC
Chambersburg PA
CBHW081059180526
45170CB00005B/1815
9780359972043